Quantum Transformation

Guide to Becoming a Galactic Human

John Hornecker

LIFE SCIENCES CENTER

Quantum Transformation

ISBN 978-0-9627270-1-6

Life Sciences Center
P. O. Box 504
Lake Lure, NC 28746

Printed in USA by 48HrBooks (www.48HrBooks.com)

A Choice

We are at the threshold of a quantum shift in human evolution. The opportunity that is opening to each of us, and to all of us, collectively, is unprecedented in the history of Earth.

A cosmic doorway is opening. We have the opportunity to step through it into our fullness as a 'galactic human,' or to remain behind within the third dimensional world of duality to experience another vast cycle of struggle between good and evil.

The choice is for each of us to make – no one can make it for us. It is a choice that will define our individual destiny for millennia to come.

This is a guidebook for those who choose to step forward and embark on the path to becoming a 'galactic human.'

Dedication

This book is dedicated to the advanced souls who have courageously been coming into human embodiment during the past few decades to provide leadership for humanity as we emerge from the great shift that is taking place here on Earth. Sometimes referred to as the Indigo, Crystal and Rainbow children, many of these souls have retained conscious awareness of their spiritual nature and the mission they have come to fulfill.

Table of Contents

Part IV - Becoming a Galactic Human

Appendix

Introduction

Life abounds throughout all of Creation. Planet Earth is only one of countless worlds that are home to conscious beings. Each planetary system is unique, providing an opportunity for experiences that will further our evolutionary development. In this sense, each is like a university, with its own particular 'curriculum.'

Earth was designed to be a planet of exquisite beauty, with a vast diversity of life-forms. And all of us who have come here have come to learn about LOVE – in all of its forms – within the context of great diversity.

Everything within Creation is cyclical in nature. Earth is completing a cycle of evolutionary experience, a cycle that began long, long ago. Part of the grand design is that at the end of each such cycle, there is an opportunity for all who have successfully progressed through the learning experiences to 'graduate,' and move upward on the evolutionary spiral to the next developmental opportunity.

Earth, herself, is a conscious, living being that is evolving as all inhabited planets do. As planets evolve, they ascend to increasingly higher frequencies, which is another way of saying that they become less dense. Earth is currently a 3rd dimensional planet, and she is in the process of transforming into a 4th, and then 5th dimensional planet.

At this point, a note of clarification may be helpful. Earth is sometimes referred to as a 3rd 'density' planet, rather than a 3rd 'dimensional' planet. In this sense, the words 'dimension' and 'density' are often used interchangeably. This tends to add an element of confusion, especially since Albert Einstein referred to 'dimension' in a very different context. He spoke of 'time' being the 4th dimension of our time-space reality. However, since the term 'dimension' is so commonly used in reference to the evolutionary level of planetary systems, we will generally use that term rather than 'density,' even though 'density' is perhaps a more descriptive term.

9

As galaxies and universes evolve, it is essential that each of the celestial systems within them evolve in appropriate relationship to each other. There is a modest range of tolerance in this regard, but there are limits as to the degree of variance that can be accommodated. For reasons which will be discussed later in this book, Planet Earth has been lagging substantially behind in its evolutionary progress, and is currently the densest inhabited planet in our entire universe.

It is not just Earth that is nearing the end of a long cycle of evolution; our entire universe is simultaneously completing a vast cycle of cosmic evolution! However, in order for our universe to be able to graduate to the next higher level on the evolutionary scale, Earth must transition from the 3rd dimension to the 5th dimension. It has been decreed by the Creator of our universe that *this will happen*!

For all who live on Earth, this provides an unprecedented opportunity, an opportunity to ascend along with her to the 5th dimension. However, within our universe the principle of 'free will' is sacred. Each of us who resides on Earth at this time must choose either to ascend with Earth, or to remain within the 3rd dimension. And in fact, *unless we make the choice to ascend, the 'default' choice is to remain at the 3rd dimensional level.*

But ascension requires more than just a simple choice; it requires focused and dedicated effort to prepare for this shift in frequency. Much of this book deals with some of the processes that are involved. The words in the sub-title of this book – "becoming a galactic human"– imply coming into the fullness of the divine being that we are, and taking our rightful place as a citizen of our galaxy. This is the path of ascension.

Of course, there is much about the near-term future that we do not know. In this book we will speculate on some of the possibilities. But above all else, there is one thing about which we can be absolutely certain – the more that we open our hearts and incorporate LOVE into every aspect of our daily lives, the better prepared we will be for whatever the future holds.

Part I

Spiritual Awakening

and

Transformation

Chapter 1

Awakening

As we come into human embodiment through the birth process, virtually all of our early life experiences are in the context of our *human* self. Most profound, of course, are our relationships with our mother and father, from whom we derive our physical sustenance and emotional nurturance.

Then, as we grow from infancy into the toddler years, we continue to relate to others in our lives, such as siblings or other relatives and friends, as physical beings that we experience mostly through our five senses. As our personalities gradually develop, our relationships with others are heavily influenced by human personality factors.

As we progress through our educational years, the goals and values upon which our emerging lives are based tend to be from a human perspective: obtaining a good education that will support our career choices, finding a loving and compatible life partner, procuring a pleasant home and planning for financial security. Virtually all of these are related to our *human* nature.

Somewhere along the way, however, many of us begin to look beyond human fulfillment. We begin to explore feelings from somewhere deep within – feelings that there must be something more to life than that which we can see and touch. For some, this may be inspired by a religious experience. Or, we may be struggling with disappointments over plans that didn't work out the way that we had anticipated. For others, it may be a personal injury or illness, perhaps the death of a friend or family member that drives us to a deeper search for what life is *really* all about.

In some cases, the 'wake-up' call may be of a different form, such as a dream or vision that gets our attention. Or maybe we have an intuitive hunch or premonition that later proves to be accurate.

Synchronicities can also play an important role. Perhaps we are driving along a highway while in a quandary about an issue in our life, and then suddenly we pass a billboard with words or images that seem to speak directly to our situation. Or maybe we have been thinking about a friend with whom we have been out of touch for several years, and then suddenly 'out of the blue' we receive a telephone call or e-mail from them.

Such experiences seem to reach beyond our rational minds, and bring into play aspects of life that can't be explained or understood in simply *human* terms.

If we are fortunate, a book or magazine that offers relevant insights may show up in our life. Or perhaps we unexpectedly meet someone who is having similar experiences. We may see a flyer on a bulletin board that describes an upcoming lecture or workshop that seems to speak to our issues or questions. Invariably, once our mind begins to open to new perspectives and possibilities, we will draw to us the insights and guidance we seek.

Our Higher Self

The reality is that we are, indeed, much more than the human form that we see in the mirror. We are 'spiritual' beings that are here on Earth having a 'human' experience. At our most fundamental level of existence, we are an individualization of the essence of our Creator. Sometimes this is referred to as a 'Divine Spark;' or in esoteric terms, our 'I AM Presence' or 'Monad.' Regardless of the label we use, it is an individualized aspect of our Creator that remains ever connected to our Creator. It is eternal, and at One with all of Creation. We will simply refer to it as our 'Higher Self.'

Our Higher Self is all-Loving and all-Wise. It is continually evolving through experiences within various realms of Creation. Our Higher Self also has been gifted with access to the creative power of our Creator.

14

Our Soul and Oversoul

Our soul and oversoul are essentially an intermediate level that exists between our Higher Self and our human self, as depicted in the diagram. Whereas our Higher Self is the individualized essence of our Creator and remains in a state of perfection, our soul and oversoul embody the totality of our cumulative life experiences. At the end of each lifetime, whether here on Earth or within some other realm, the memory of our experiences is integrated into our soul and oversoul.

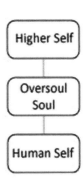

What is the difference between our soul and our oversoul? Sometimes the analogy of a human hand is used to describe the relationship between them. The fleshy part of the hand would represent the oversoul, while a soul would be represented by one of the fingers. This obviously implies that there is more than one soul associated with a particular oversoul, and that is indeed true. This will be discussed in more detail in Chapter 10.

Life plan

Prior to entering into a new life experience here on Earth, our soul and oversoul, in concert with our Higher Self and our guides and mentors, create a 'life plan' for our upcoming life experience. As part of this planning process, we also work out 'soul agreements' with other souls who agree to play a significant role in our upcoming life.

Free will

Upon entering into human embodiment, we normally do not retain memory of our life plan within our conscious mind. Rather, we are given 'free will' to make choices and decisions as we go about our daily life. As we experience the results of those choices, we have an opportunity to learn and grow.

Like a watchful parent, however, our soul closely monitors our human life. A considerable amount of latitude is built into most life plans, so our soul does not intervene as long as we progress within the general framework of the plan. But if we begin to make choices that take us too far off course, our soul will step in.

At first, the guidance from our soul is usually in the form of a 'gentle nudge.' We may begin to feel uncomfortable about a decision we have made or about the way things are beginning to unfold in our life. Often this is in the form of an 'intuitive' feeling. If we are responsive to these feelings and begin to make adjustments in the direction our life has been heading, then our soul will step back as we work through the changes in our life.

Soul intervention

However, if we continue to ignore the 'gentle nudges,' our soul will be somewhat more forceful in the manner in which it intercedes. Maybe we will become ill or have a minor accident that blocks us from going ahead with an activity we had planned. Perhaps there will be a break-up in a relationship that we had been pursuing, but which is not in our highest good. Or possibly we will lose our job, which will then force us to explore other opportunities.

Being in the 'flow'

The whole point is that our life can be a lot more joyful and harmonious if we learn to respond to the 'gentle nudges' from our soul, rather than ignoring them and thus inviting intervention of a more dramatic nature. As we begin to better understand this process, we gradually learn to be more sensitive to the flow of our life. If we encounter obstacles or resistance related to something we are attempting to do, then it is probably time to step back and check our inner feelings. Another way of saying this – it would be well to listen to the promptings from our soul.

Chapter 2

Living from Our Heart

Most of our human experiences and cultural conditioning tend to focus on the importance of our mind, our cognitive thought processes. Certainly our educational system is almost totally directed toward mental activity. We learn to use logic and reasoning, and we are taught to deal with 'factual' information.

So it is only natural that as we live our human life, it tends to be directed by what we are *thinking*, rather than by what we are *feeling*.

One of the most fundamental aspects of our spiritual awakening and transformation is to shift from our *head* to our *heart* – to learn to rely on the feelings within our heart, rather than the thoughts in our head when we are faced with an important life decision.

For reasons which will be discussed in much more detail later in this book, our heart is the aspect of our human self that is most deeply in touch with our soul and our Higher Self.

On the other hand, our thoughts are most powerfully impacted by our cultural conditioning: by what we have learned from our parents, by what we have been taught in school or in church, by what we see on television or read in a newspaper or book, by the thoughts and attitudes of our friends, by the mindset and behavioral patterns that are expected of us related to our work, and yes, by the internet and its social networks. All of these inform our thinking as a *human*. But virtually none of them take into consideration who we are as a *spiritual being*. For this, we need to turn to our heart.

One of the most difficult challenges associated with spiritual transformation is learning to let go of 'old thinking,' of 'old attitudes' that are based on distorted ideas or outdated cultural frameworks. It is only when we turn to our heart that we begin to learn to live our life based on spiritual awareness, on deep inner knowingness.

Chapter 3

New Insights into the Human Heart

In the past few years, several new discoveries have been made about the human heart. Perhaps the most profound of these is that within the fatty tissue surrounding the heart, especially at the base of the heart, are neural networks that are virtually identical to the neural networks within our brain. This has given rise to the realization that our heart essentially has its own 'brain.' Moreover, we are learning that some of the important functions which previously had been thought to be performed by the brain in our head, actually are directed from within our 'heart-brain.'

One of the organizations that has been actively involved in this new area of research is the Institute of HeartMath, located in Boulder Creek, California.[1] Central to their work has been an effort to better understand the functional relationship between our heart-brain and the brain in our head, and also to explore the role that our emotions play in these interactions.

Additional insights about the heart can be gained by exploring the way the human body is originally formed. Starting with the original female egg that is fertilized by the male sperm to create a zygote, the zygote then splits into two cells through the process of mitosis. Then, the 2 cells each split into 2 cells, forming a group of 4. Finally, each cell in the group of 4 splits to form a group of 8 cells, which is cubic in shape. Such a group of 8 cells is the basic building block of all biological life forms. In the case of the development of a human, the next step is for each of the 8 cells to go through a similar process to become 8 building blocks of 8 cells each, or a total of 64 cells. And then it goes through another iteration of this process to form into a cluster of 512 cells, all of which are part of the emerging human heart. Yes, at this point *the entire developing organism that will eventually become the fetus is part of what will become the heart*! And furthermore, at this point of development, *this emerging heart begins to beat!*[2]

Researchers have long been puzzled as to how the heart can begin to beat before there has been any development of the brain. The heart is the only organ in the body that seems to 'march to its own drummer.' It has its own pacemaker cells which control the rate at which the heart beats. Because of this, a common saying among researchers has historically been that the heart seems to have a 'mind of its own.' Now, with the discovery that the heart does, indeed, have its own 'brain,' this reference to a 'mind of its own' takes on a new and more profound meaning.

Further, researchers are coming to realize that it is the heart, more specifically the heart-brain, that synchronizes much of the functioning of the brain in our head. Research at HeartMath has centered on this synchronization role, and the manner in which our emotions and various other factors enhance or inhibit this process.

Not surprisingly, research has shown that emotional states, such as frustration, anxiety or anger, introduce chaos into the synchronization process, and thus inhibit our cognitive thinking ability. On the other hand, it has been demonstrated that harmonious emotional states tend to optimize synchronization, thus maximizing our cognitive abilities. It has been discovered that one of the emotions that has the most powerful positive impact on synchronization is that of 'appreciation.'

HeartMath researchers have adopted the term 'coherence' to indicate an emotional state of being that enhances the synchronization process. They have developed numerous techniques and processes for helping people learn to achieve and maintain a state of coherence.

Insights gained through heart transplants

One of the fascinating aspects of these new discoveries related to the heart-brain involves the experiences of people who have undergone heart transplants. Appendix A includes some specific examples.

It would be naïve to draw any specific conclusions based on a very limited number of cases. It is an area in which credible research could prove to be very insightful. However, the stories that we have included in Appendix A suggest some interesting possibilities as to the role of the heart-brain related to:

- Personality characteristics
- Feelings about people
- Food preferences
- Activity preferences

They also suggest that when we make reference to the 'desires of the heart,' we may well be referring to information and feelings that are stored within the heart-brain. Sometimes common sayings carry wisdom that goes unnoticed by our cognitive mind. For example when we say "I love you from the bottom of my heart," are we really referring to our heart-brain which resides primarily in the fatty tissue at the base of the heart? These are interesting possibilities to ponder.

The heart – an electromagnetic generator

The heart is by far the most powerful electromagnetic generator in the body. The electromagnetic field as measured by an electrocardiogram (ECG) is about <u>60</u> times greater than *brain waves* recorded by an electroencephalogram (EEG). And, the *magnetic component* of the heart's field is approximately <u>5,000</u> times stronger than that produced by the brain. This electromagnetic field is not impeded by tissue, and can be measured several feet away from the body. This has significant implications related to the process we use to draw into our life that which we desire. In Chapter 6, we will discuss this in greater detail.

Chapter 4

Intuition – Listening to Our Soul

Virtually everyone has had experiences with intuition. It may be an idea that suddenly comes to us from 'out of the blue.' Perhaps we have been grappling with a difficult situation in our life, and then we awaken one morning and feel a sense of clarity about how to proceed. Or, it may be a feeling we have about a business associate we have recently met, such as whether or not they are trustworthy.

A few decades ago there was a lot of interest in 'brain mapping;' in distinguishing the functions that take place in the left cerebral hemisphere from those that take place in the right hemisphere. The logical, rational, structured aspect of thinking is associated with the left-brain, whereas the less structured, more spontaneous and imaginative thinking is associated with the right-brain. Most of the researchers associated the function of 'intuition' with the right-brain. But my own sense has been that it is not correct to associate the function of 'intuition' with either the right-brain or the left-brain – that *intuition is not a cerebral function.*

Throughout the intervening years, additional insights about intuition have come to me, but it was not until the discovery of the heart-brain that everything began to fall into place.

Our heart mind

Later in this book, we will discuss the bio-mechanics of intuition in more depth. But for now, we will simply state that intuition is primarily communication from our soul, and it comes into our awareness through our heart-brain, or heart-mind.

Although the words 'brain' and 'mind' tend to be used somewhat interchangeably, at this point we would like to make a distinction. Using the analogy of a computer, our 'brain' is like the computer 'hardware,' whereas our 'mind' is akin to the 'software.' Just as computer software functions through the hardware, so also our mind functions through our brain, whether it be the brain in our head, or the brain that is associated with our heart.

One of the important differences between intuition and cognitive thinking is that we are not in conscious control of the functioning of intuition in the same way we are with cognitive thinking. So in order to expand our intuitive abilities, we need to pay attention to the times and situations in which our intuition seems to be most active. Following are some of the situations in which many people find that intuition seems to flow most easily:

- As we are awakening from sleep, in quietness and before our conscious mind becomes active.
- While we are taking a shower or bath; there seems to be something about water flowing over us that stimulates our intuition.
- When we are doing something repetitive that does not require much conscious thought, such as washing dishes, driving a car on an un-crowded highway, or going for a walk.
- When we are 'day-dreaming' and our conscious mind is quiet and unfocused.
- When we are writing, either by hand or using a word processor.

By paying attention to your own daily activities and rhythms, you will soon learn when intuition is most active for you.

Transition from sleep to wakefulness

The first situation that is listed – the transition from sleep to wakefulness – is such a fertile opportunity for intuitive flow that we want to discuss it in some depth.

In that in-between state in which we are still partially asleep and just beginning to awaken, we seem to have the ability to be in touch with elements of both states of being, and we can drift back and forth between the two. There may be remnants of a dream that was part of our sleep-state experience, or there may be thoughts or ideas that seem to find their way into our awareness from some unknown place. It is best to just allow our mind to stay in a state of 'unfocused awareness' for a while so that the flow will continue.

Through experience, we can learn to linger in this transition zone for extended periods of time. The trick is to hang on to the seed-thoughts (intuitive flashes) that percolate out of this in-between state of being. The act of writing them down or recording them with a voice recorder usually brings us too far over into the wakeful state, making it difficult to return to the in-between zone. But we can learn to engage our conscious mind just enough to capture the seed-thoughts as they arise, and then when we feel that our experience is 'complete,' we can gently move into wakefulness and jot down or record the key thoughts or ideas.

The in-between state between sleep and wakefulness is sometimes referred to as an 'interstitial' zone, as discussed in more depth in Appendix B.

Active and sharply focused cerebral thinking is the enemy of intuition; it tends to block out or override an intuitive flow, which is of a much more subtle nature. One way to counter this is to set aside periods of time throughout an active day to 'de-focus' our mind. An analogy may be helpful.

Most people are familiar with the concept of 'de-focusing' our eyes, and just look with a 'soft gaze.' When we do this, we are often able to see things with our peripheral vision that disappear when we sharpen the focus of our eyes. Intuition functions in a similar way – when we de-focus our conscious mind, we enable intuition to come through. This process is very similar to 'daydreaming.'

In the last chapter we discussed the importance of being in a state of 'coherence,' or emotional harmony, for our mind to function at its maximum effectiveness.   This applies even more so to the flow of intuition through our heart-mind.

Chapter 5

Our Guides and Guardian Angels

Each of us has a guardian angel who was assigned to us before our birth. Their role is to watch over us and protect us throughout our life. We also have guides and mentors who are available to assist us from the unseen realms. However, they are all severely restricted as to the extent they are permitted to assist us unless we *ask for their help.* This is because of the 'principle of non-interference.'

Simply stated, the principle of non-interference says that a being within our universe is not permitted to intervene in the affairs of someone in a lesser evolved world unless they are invited to do so. The purpose for this is to assure that we are not deprived of our learning opportunities. In this sense, it is very much like a parent watching over a child. We know it is important for children to learn to do things for themselves, and so a parent normally does not intervene unless they see that a child is going to be in danger if they proceed with what they are doing.

So one of the most important things we can do, especially as we move through the spiritual transformation process, is to *ask for assistance.* It is also important, when we sense that assistance is being provided, to thank the beings who are helping us, even if we do not know specifically from whom or where the assistance is coming. Learning to live with a grateful heart is a profoundly important aspect of our spiritual development.

Beings within the higher realms are able to observe our life situations from a much broader perspective than is available to us while we are in a human body. Sometimes that which we, from our human perspective, might be inclined to ask for may not necessarily be in our best interest if viewed from a higher perspective. So when we ask for help, it is a good idea to always qualify the request with the phrase 'so long as it is in my highest good and the highest good for all who are involved.'

Within the angelic realm are angels that specialize in many different forms of service. *Healing* is certainly a primary area of service. *Protection* is another one. As we begin to interact with the angels on a regular basis in our daily life, it is amazing how much easier and more harmonious our life can become!

Assistance from our guides and mentors can come to us in many different ways. Guidance often comes to us in a manner that is similar to an intuitive flow. In fact, we might not be able to distinguish the difference, especially in the early stages of our spiritual awakening.

Chapter 6

Using Our Creative Power Wisely

We are constantly creating the experiences and situations that show up in our life day by day. Since most people do not understand how the creative process works, the experiences that arrive at their doorstep tend to be a hodgepodge, all too often a mixture of circumstances and incidents that they would prefer not to encounter. The tendency is to blame their life situations on 'bad luck.' Or worse yet, they eventually perceive themselves to be 'unworthy' of goodness and abundance in their life.

Learning to use our creative power wisely is an important step in our spiritual transformation. Once again it is our *heart* that is at the center of this creative process, and it is our *intentions* that are the key.

The spiritual principle that is involved is sometimes referred to as the 'law of attraction.' Simply stated, this law says that we attract into our life that which resonates with our thoughts and emotions. If we are constantly focusing on the problems in our life, we attract more of the same. If we continually focus on 'lack' – lack of money, lack of a good job, lack of a love relationship, lack of good health – we will draw to us more of the same. The law of attraction assures it.

The key to changing our life experiences is to learn to focus on what we *want* in our life, rather than on what we *don't want*.

In discussing some of the recent discoveries related to the human heart, we indicated that the heart is a very powerful electromagnetic generator. Through it we constantly radiate our thoughts and emotions out from us in all directions. Consequently, in accordance with the law of attraction, we attract to us the experiences, the people, the situations which resonate with the thoughts and emotions that we are sending out.

An analogy may be helpful. Consider a radio broadcasting station. The radio wave that is broadcast out from the antenna at the top of the tower is electromagnetic energy. Before the radio wave is sent to the antenna, it is *modulated* (encoded) with the programming being created in the radio studio. It may be a news broadcast, it may be music, or it may be a wide range of other programming with which we are all generally familiar.

At the receiving end is a radio receiver that is able to *demodulate* (decode) the radio wave and retrieve the programming information that originated in the studio. Additionally, as we know, a radio receiver can be tuned to any particular radio station. So the person with the radio receiver can select the radio station that has the type of programming to which they are attracted. The people who are attracted to a radio station that is broadcasting a radical talk-show host are likely to be quite different from the people who are attracted to a station that is broadcasting an orchestral rendition of Grieg's 'Morning' from the Peer Gynt suite. In the first case, the people who are attracted will be those who resonate with hatred and bigotry. In the second case, the people who are attracted would tend to be those who resonate with joy and inspiration.

Returning now to a consideration of our own 'broadcasting station' – our heart – the people and the related experiences that will be drawn to us all depend on the 'programming' that we are broadcasting out from our heart. If we are angry, then more anger will be attracted to us. If we are judgmental toward others, then judgmental people will be drawn to us. If we are fearful, then fearful situations will find us. However, if we are joyful and upbeat, then we will attract people who also are joyful and upbeat. If we are kind and generous to others, then kindness and generosity will be attracted into our life.

The power of our intentions

It is through the nature of our *intentions* that we create the 'program content' which is modulated into the electromagnetic wave that is radiated out to the world from our heart. This may seem like a simple statement, but its implications are profound.

Intentions have both *thought* and *emotional* components. *Thought* energy is *electric* in nature, whereas *emotional* energy is *magnetic.* Combining thought and emotion creates a 'hybrid' that we call 'intention,' just as the combining of electric energy with magnetic energy creates a hybrid field that we call 'electromagnetic.' To summarize this for clarity's sake:

Electric energy + Magnetic energy = Electromagnetic energy
Thought   +   Emotion   = Intention

Since the awareness of the heart-brain is quite recent, researchers are only at the very early stages of understanding the various ways in which it functions. Based on what we know so far, we can intuit a functional model as to how we go about forming our intentions, and then modulating those intentions into the powerful electromagnetic wave that is broadcast out to the world by our heart.

Creating and sending out an intention

Let's walk through an example of how to create and send out an intention. Let's say that an intention that you want to create at the beginning of a day is as follows:

"It is my intention to be kind to each person whom I encounter this day."

You would begin by focusing your attention on your heart, especially your heart-brain. Next, it would be helpful to take in a deep breath, hold it for a moment, and then relax and let the breath flow out. Take a couple more deep breaths in the same way. This helps to still the conscious mind and bring one's emotions into harmony.

Now, holding your focus on your heart-brain, repeat the intention statement that is highlighted above. Get in touch with the *feeling* of kindness, what it feels like when someone is kind to you, and what it feels like when you are kind to someone else.

31

Next, shift the focus of your attention to the brain in your head and form the 'thought' that is reflected in the intention. You might envision someone you are likely to encounter, and in your mind's eye, 'see' yourself being kind to them.

Then bring your attention back to your heart-brain, and feel the resonant alignment (coherence) between the thought in your head and the feeling in your heart.

While holding the *feeling* and the *thought* of kindness, speak the intention statement slowly and clearly. Then say, **"So it is."** As you say, "So it is," release the intention through your heart and envision your heart broadcasting it out to the world.

As you move through your day and are 'intentionally' kind to each person you encounter, it will reinforce your awareness and add energy to the intention.

As with anything new, the process of creating and sending forth an intention may seem a bit awkward or cumbersome the first few times you do it, but it will soon become second nature. Then you can more easily focus on the power of the thought and feeling of the intention that you are creating and sending out.

The principle is quite simple. It is learning to be *consistently* aware of the programming that we are sending out into the world that requires some attention. Remember, our heart broadcast not just when we are consciously thinking about it, it broadcasts ALL OF THE TIME – 24 hours a day – every day of the year!

Changing our 'attitudes'

On a human personality level, we are familiar with the concept of having an 'attitude.' We say that Joe has a '*bad attitude*' or Suzie has a '*good attitude.*' These are, of course, patterns of thinking and emotional behavior. These patterns, good or bad, are constantly being broadcast out into the world around us.

Regardless as to where we are on the scale, we can begin to improve or transform our attitude through our intentions. As we create and use statements of intention, such as the following:

"I intend to be helpful and courteous to people that I meet"

"I intend to experience and express joy in my life"

"I intend to be generous to others"

we will find our attitude toward life beginning to shift. We also will become more consciously aware of those moments or incidents in which we are not acting in alignment with our intentions.

Through such a process, the nature of the thoughts and feelings that we broadcast out into the world will become more consistently positive. Consequently, we will find that the people, the experiences, and the situations that we attract into our life will shift accordingly. As we begin to experience these positive shifts, it will provide encouragement and reinforcement to a growing awareness that, no matter what our situations or behavior patterns have been in the past, we can indeed take positive control and create our life the way we want it to be.

Chapter 7

A Healthy Body

An essential aspect of spiritual transformation involves our physical body. Evolution is all about raising our frequency as we deepen our connection with our Higher Self and assimilate more Light into our beingness. An unhealthy body can be a serious deterrent to our progress.

Natural health

Restoring the natural health of our body involves three fundamental elements:

- Cleansing our internal organs such as our liver, gallbladder, kidneys and colon so that they can perform their functions efficiently.
- Shifting to a diet of natural foods, including fruits, vegetables, grains and nuts, and drinking ample quantities of fresh water.
- Adopting a healthy lifestyle that includes exercise, emotional balance and regular sleep patterns.

Many of our cultural habits in the Western world work in opposition to a healthy body. This situation is exacerbated by medical practices that rely heavily on medications and surgery.

The medical term for illnesses that are caused by the medical profession is 'iatrogenic.' It is difficult to obtain accurate data on the extent of this problem because of potential litigation issues. However, a

10-year study of government statistics completed in 2003 concluded that iatrogenic illness was the leading cause of death in the United States.[3]

It is up to each of us to learn how to care for our own body. Unfortunately, most of the information with which we are bombarded on a daily basis is provided by companies that are interested in selling us products or services, rather than helping us understand how to keep our bodies healthy.

The human body has amazing resiliency and recuperative powers. If we work in cooperation with the natural functioning of our body, it is seldom too late to make changes that will restore our health and vitality.

Internal cleansing

From an early age most of us are taught about the importance of good hygiene, the *external* cleanliness of our body. However, we are seldom taught about the importance of keeping our body clean on the *inside* as well.

Our liver, the largest organ in our body, is responsible for processing, distributing and maintaining the body's 'fuel supply.' Another function of the liver is to break down alcohol and other toxic substances, including bacteria, parasites and various drug compounds. More than a quart of blood is filtered through the liver every minute, removing toxins and distributing nutrients throughout the body.

Our liver also produces *bile*, which is essential to our digestive process. The gallbladder serves as a reservoir for bile so that adequate amounts of it are available when needed.

One of the most common health problem involves the formation of hardened 'stones' within the liver and gallbladder. These stones, ranging in size from a kernel of grain to a large pea, form as a result of an unhealthy diet and lifestyle. When the liver and gallbladder become congested with these stones, which unfortunately is very common, all of the functions of the liver and gallbladder become impaired.

The good news is that these stones can be removed from the liver and gallbladder through a simple and inexpensive series of cleanses. And by maintaining a healthy diet and lifestyle, the liver and gallbladder can be restored to a healthy state of functioning.

36

A similar situation frequently exists with our kidneys. The main responsibility of the kidneys is to keep the blood pure and healthy, maintain proper fluid balance within the body, and release toxins through the urine. If the kidneys become congested, they are not able to adequately separate out the toxins from the blood.

Various herbs can be effectively and painlessly used to dissolve congestion within the kidneys and restore their healthy functioning within a period of 3 to 6 weeks.

Information on how to do a liver and gallbladder cleanse or a kidney cleanse is available in the book, *The Amazing Liver and Gallbladder Flush* by Andreas Moritz.[4]

One more aspect of internal hygiene is very important and that relates to our intestinal tract (colon). Our body's health and vitality depend on thorough elimination of waste products from our intestinal tract. Many physical problems are caused by a build-up of waste material that may at first accumulate in the large intestine, and then spread to other parts of the body. Chronic situations are a common cause of colon cancer.

Colon hydrotherapy, also called 'colonic irrigation' or simply 'colonic,' is one of the most effective colon therapies. Within a short period of time, a colonic can eliminate large amounts of trapped waste that may have taken many years to accumulate. A typical colonic session takes a little less than an hour, and is available in most locations throughout the country.

The importance of drinking water

Dehydration of the body is one of the most common health problems. Drinking sufficient quantities of water at appropriate times throughout the day is probably the single most important thing we can do to improve our health.

Virtually all of the organs and systems within the human body require adequate amounts of water in order to function properly. When there is dehydration, metabolic waste products cannot be removed properly. Drinking sufficient amounts of fresh water is an essential prerequisite for avoiding disease and slowing the aging process.

Healthy Nutrition

Healthy nutrition involves a return to the simple gifts of nature: fresh vegetables, delicious fruits, tasty seeds and nuts. Unfortunately, the diet of the majority of people in the Western world consists predominately of 'processed' foods. Typical problems with processed foods are:

- They are infused with harmful preservatives in order to increase 'shelf life.'
- They tend to be laden with unhealthy sugars, sweeteners and salts, designed to appeal to our taste buds, but which are detrimental to our body.
- Meat and meat products are usually derived from animals that have been fed or injected with large quantities of antibiotics, growth stimulants and other substances, all of which are designed to maximize production on 'factory farms.' Also, many meat products are contaminated with illness-producing bacteria, such as Salmonella or E. coli.
- Some food products are 'irradiated' in order to kill bacteria and promote shelf life, resulting in foods that are lifeless and lacking in nutritional value.
- Processed foods are frequently prepared by cooking them in oil that contains significant quantities of polyunsaturated fats, resulting in food that is unhealthy for the body.
- Many types of processed foods are prepared and packaged in such a way as to be conveniently heated in a microwave oven. Microwave cooking kills enzymes and other important nutrients, leaving essentially 'dead' food that has little nutritional value.

A diet that consists primarily of processed foods is often referred to as the Standard American Diet, or 'SAD.' The acronym says it all!

On the other hand, natural foods, if they are grown and prepared properly, and eaten when they are fresh, tend to provide the nutrients and life forces that are needed for a healthy body.

Unfortunately, modern commercial agricultural practices tend to work against the production of healthy, natural foods. There is often an over-reliance on the use of chemical fertilizers and pesticides to increase food production. Such chemicals tend to find their way into the fibers of the resulting vegetables, fruits and other agricultural products.

The emergence of organic farming is an effort to move back to more natural agricultural methods that do not rely on chemicals. Originally, 'natural' food stores were the most common source of organic food products. However, as consumer awareness has heightened, organic fruits and vegetables are now being sold in 'specialty' sections of the produce department in most mainstream supermarkets.

Also, within the past several years, the number of 'farmers markets,' has increased dramatically, enabling local farmers to sell their produce directly to consumers. Usually these are set up on a one-day per week basis, such as Saturday. There is no guarantee that such produce is free of chemical contamination, but the likelihood is that the produce grown on small local farms will be much more nutritious than that produced on commercial mega-farms.

There has been an ongoing debate as to whether it is better to eat vegetables and fruits raw or cooked. Since heating foods kills enzymes and alters other nutrients, it would seem that eating a diet of nothing but raw natural food would be ideal. But it is not quite that simple.

Raw vegetables do not pass through the digestive tract as easily as cooked vegetables, and sometimes the intestines can become congested. On the other hand, cooked vegetables are much less likely to overwhelm the colon. Hence, an appropriate balance between raw and cooked vegetables is probably the best approach.

Another good alternative is to put raw vegetables through a food juicer, and then drink the vegetable juice. This insures a good supply of natural enzymes without over-burdening the digestive system.

Sprouts are another good addition. They can be easily grown at home, and with careful planning, they can be grown in just the right quantity so that they can always be eaten while they are still very fresh.

We would be remiss if we did not comment on the hazards associated with microwave cooking. Microwave ovens were originally developed in Nazi Germany during WWII to simplify the logistics of feeding armies on the move. After the war was over, both the Soviet Union and the Western countries obtained the technology, including documentation related to testing that had been done by the Germans. The Soviets were so alarmed by the test results that they banned the use of microwave ovens in the Soviet Union for several decades.

In the West, extensive testing was eventually done in Switzerland, but again, the results were very disturbing – so disturbing that a trade association of manufacturing companies filed legal action and was successful in suppressing the data for several years.[5]

Two primary concerns are involved: the microwave radiation while the oven is turned on, and the effect that microwave cooking has on the food. It is the latter that is of the greatest concern. The safest approach is simply to avoid the use of microwave cooking.

Healthy lifestyle

Lifestyle is at least as important to our health as internal hygiene and nutrition.

We all know the importance of exercise. Some people get sufficient exercise in the course of their daily work, but most of us with a more sedentary lifestyle need to incorporate additional exercise in order to maintain a healthy body. The optimum type and amount of exercise naturally varies according to age, body type, and a variety of other factors. A 70-year old person does not need the same type or amount of exercise as a 20-year old. It is best to exercise during daylight hours. Vigorous exercise in the evening hours is not healthy because the body needs to slow down to prepare itself for a restful and rejuvenating sleep.

The negative impact that smoking has on our health has received so much attention during the past few decades that there is no need to dwell on that here. It is clear by now that the detrimental effects of smoking are caused not just from the tobacco, but also from a long litany of chemicals that are added to cigarettes, thus drugging the body and creating addiction. Simply stated, smoking is incompatible with good health.

The biological processes within our bodies are synchronized to the daily cycles of light and darkness. By understanding the nature of these cycles and adjusting our daily lives accordingly, we can better support our body's natural biological functions. As we intuitively know, the hours of darkness are the time our body does most of its cleansing and rejuvenation.

Sleep is an essential part of this cyclical process. Sleep can be divided into two main parts: *before* midnight and *after* midnight. The most important processes of purification and renewal occur during the two hours of sleep *before* midnight. This period involves deep sleep that typically lasts for about an hour, from 11 pm to midnight. During this period, one enters a dreamless state of sleep in which oxygen consumption in the body drops considerably. This results in profound physical rest and relaxation. The benefit to your body of this single hour of deep sleep is approximately equivalent to that derived during the three hours after midnight, when the oxygen consumption rises again.

Structuring our daily lives in a way that honors our body's natural cycles is one of the most important things we can do to enhance our health and well-being. Of course, situations occasionally arise in life that necessitate making exceptions to our normal daily cycle. However, the more consistently we maintain a regular pattern of living, the better we are able to support our body's natural processes of regeneration.

Perhaps less obvious are the effects that our thoughts and emotions have on our health. Stress, anger, resentment and frustration all interfere with the healthy functioning of our body's organs and systems. On the other hand, love, joy and happiness all have a positive impact on our health and well-being.

Stress is one of the greatest deterrents to health. Virtually all of us experience stress in our lives from time to time, and our bodies are designed to respond accordingly. For example, if we encounter physical danger, the 'fight or flight' stress responses within our body are designed to help us protect ourselves from that danger. So long as experiences of this nature are not frequent, our body is generally able to restore its normal equilibrium without any significant long-term effect on our health.

The more damaging situations are those to which we are exposed on an ongoing basis, such as a stressful work situation, an inharmonious relationship or constant worries related to finances. Even watching the daily television news programs tend to create levels of stress within us as we react emotionally to situations that seem tragic or unjust.

Fortunately, as we awaken to our spiritual nature and gradually shift the focus of our life from human goals and perspectives to living in alignment with our soul's plan and purpose, it becomes much easier to deal with life's challenging situations in less stressful ways. Body, mind, and emotions are all intricately interconnected, and our spiritual progress requires that we bring harmony to all aspects of our life.

Chapter 8

Living a Transcendent Life

As we progress in our spiritual transformation, our goal is to integrate the consciousness and the virtues of our Higher Self into our human self, so that they function as a seamless unit. Some of the inherent virtues that were bestowed upon our Higher Self at the time of creation are:

Love	Compassion	Wisdom
Courage	Generosity	Kindness
Gratitude	Joy	Curiosity
Imagination	Beauty	Creativity

These are qualities which characterize a human life when it is lived to its fullest and best – a transcendent life.

Gratitude and Love

Although all of the virtues have an important place in our life, the virtues of 'love' and 'gratitude' can provide an important foundation upon which to build a transcendent life.

A powerful way to integrate 'gratitude' into our life is to set aside a few minutes at the beginning of each day, to sit quietly and thank our Higher Self for the things in our life for which we are grateful. We could start with the basics – life itself, the air we breathe, the water, the sun that lights and warms our days, the stars in the night sky, the beauty of the

Earth. Then there is our family, our friends, a place to live, food to eat, and so it goes.

Again at night, before we go to sleep, we could take a few minutes to reflect on the experiences of our day, and all that we have for which to be grateful.

As we take time to do this each day, it is amazing how our life begins to change. Increasingly we will find our thoughts and feelings to be in a state of gratitude. As our heart automatically broadcasts these feelings out into the world, we will attract more into our life for which to be grateful.

We can integrate 'love' in a similar way. For example, we could set aside a few minutes each day to reflect on people who are significantly involved in our life. As we envision each person, we could send love to them from our heart. We might visualize this love as a soft, glowing energy that enfolds them. It is important that we not limit our love to just those with whom we have a harmonious relationship. Rather, it is well to include people of whom we may not be particularly fond on a personality level, but who play an important role in our life.

Then, as we move through the experiences of our day, if we encounter a situation in which we are not sure what would be the best course of action, we could ask the question, "What would 'love' guide me to do?"

Non-judgment

As we experience our 'new' life emerging, there is a natural tendency to want to share our newfound insights with others, especially with those whom we care about the most. It is easy to become discouraged or even offended if those around us do not share the same excitement and enthusiasm about making changes in their lives. From our 'enlightened' perspective it may be easy to see how others are still creating havoc in their lives through their undisciplined thoughts and emotions.

But each soul is on its own journey, its own timetable. Although we can plant 'seed' ideas through our interactions with others, the most powerful way we can teach and inspire other people is through the example of our own life.

So many souls here on Earth are still firmly stuck in the human drama. Some may awaken tomorrow, some next month or next year, and some may not fully awaken in this lifetime. It is still important for us to continue to see the Divine Presence of our Creator in everyone, no matter where they are on their soul's journey or the choices they make in their life.

As we focus on our own life, it is well to remember that no matter where we are in our transformational journey, there is so much for which to be thankful and so much more yet to unfold.

Part II

Living a

Multidimensional Life

Chapter 9

Heart and Soul

Earlier, we indicated that an important first step in our spiritual awakening and transformation process is to shift our life focus from our *head* to our *heart*, from *thinking* to *feeling*. As we make this shift and gradually open our self to the promptings from our soul, our sense of purpose and direction in life increasingly becomes associated with our soul, rather than with our human self.

Important decisions in our life tend to be guided much more by our soul's mission and purpose than by our human goals and desires. We generally find that we have much less need for societal accolades and recognition in order to feel a sense of fulfillment in life. Yes, we are still very much involved in our human experience and go about our daily life – especially our relationships – in a 'heartful' manner. However, our deepest sense of satisfaction and contentment increasingly tends to be related to our soul.

As this shift occurs, most of us find it helpful to know more about our soul and oversoul, more about the ways in which we can enhance communication and connection with these aspects of our self. We seek to learn more about how we can tap into higher consciousness and experience life in the fullness of our 'Oneness' with all of creation. This is a journey which leads us toward becoming a 'galactic human,' and it is the focus of Part II of this book.

Chapter 10

Soul and Oversoul Structures

Let's explore the nature of our soul and oversoul in more depth. In an earlier chapter, we used the analogy of a human hand to describe the relationship between our soul and oversoul, with the fleshy part of our hand representing our oversoul and each finger representing a related soul. As an oversoul evolves, the structure of the oversoul progresses through several stages of development. As part of the transformation from one stage to the next, the number of souls that are associated with the oversoul increases.

One of the common soul/oversoul configurations for beings of advanced development includes 12 individual soul units. To illustrate this particular oversoul structure, let's consider the model shown in the image at the right.

If one has 13 spheres, all the same size, 12 of the spheres will fit perfectly around the 13th sphere in the center. Each of the 12 peripheral spheres is in direct contact with central 13th sphere. In this model, the center sphere would represent the oversoul, and each of the 12 peripheral spheres  would represent a soul that is an integral part of the oversoul 'cluster.'

Such an arrangement implies that more than one soul of the oversoul cluster can extend into human embodiment at the same time, thus expanding the collective experience of the oversoul cluster. The oversoul itself (sphere in the center of the cluster) does not enter into physical embodiment; it always remains within the higher realms so that it can guide the collective experience. The realm in which the oversoul resides is the 'eternal now,' which is outside of the time-space domain. So the individual soul units can, and often do, extend into embodiments that are in different time periods here on Earth.

Functioning as a 'collective'

It is possible for more than one of the souls of an oversoul cluster to extend into the same embodiment. In fact, because of the importance of this particular lifetime as Earth is completing a long evolutionary cycle, many (perhaps most) oversoul clusters are 'consolidating' into a single embodiment.

Since each soul has its own history, and therefore its own unique characteristics and sense of identity, such a consolidation can be a somewhat confusing experience from a human perspective. The human embodiment functions more as a 'collective,' with different souls of the group moving into the forefront at different times. Depending on which soul is in the forefront (driver's seat) at a particular time, we may feel like a 'different person' – indeed, we essentially are a different person!

For example, if 'Soul A' was in the forefront yesterday and 'Soul B' is in the forefront today, the personality characteristics related to 'Soul B' that we are experiencing and expressing today might be quite different from the 'Soul A' personality that we were experiencing yesterday. Also, we would tend to remember the experiences that the embodiment had yesterday with less clarity than if 'Soul A' were still in the forefront.

As is evident from this example, functioning as a collective can present challenges with regard to relationships. People who are close to you in your life, such as a life partner, may experience you as having multiple-personality issues. If your partner or a close friend is sensitive to energies, they often will see the shift in the energies in your eyes. So for them, it can be like living with a kaleidoscope – they don't quite know who (which soul) is going to be present in any given moment.

Parallel experiences

Each soul of the oversoul cluster has ongoing roles and responsibilities within the non-physical realms, whether or not it is currently in physical embodiment. For example, it may be involved in learning experiences in the 'Halls of Learning,' either as a student or a teacher, depending on the evolutionary development of the soul. Or it may be involved in a wide range of other activities. If a soul is currently projected into a human embodiment, most of these activities take place while the human body is asleep. The body in which a soul functions within the non-physical realms is sometimes referred to as a 'light body' or 'traveling body.' Even while the human body is awake, the soul continues to monitor what is going on within the non-physical realms. Sometimes it may need to partially withdraw its focus within the human self in order to carry out responsibilities in the non-physical domains. During such situations, the human self may experience drowsiness or a feeling that it is 'not all here.' Indeed, it may not be!

As we have indicated in earlier chapters, when the human self begins to awaken after it has been sleeping, there is usually a period of time before consciousness fully returns to the body, a time in which there may be 'bleed-through' of awareness from within the non-physical realms. This may be in a form similar to a dream, or it may come through as intuitive awareness. A few people who are well along in their spiritual awakening process may actually 'remember' some of what was happening in the non-physical realm.

'Non-human' soul histories

To complicate matters further, many of us have had past embodiments in forms other than human. For example, we know that the cetaceans (dolphins and whales) are sentient beings. Many of the spiritually evolved souls who are now here on Earth have had experiences as a dolphin or whale in other lifetimes. Those experiences are, of course, retained in the memory of the soul and oversoul. So in the present lifetime in a human form, such people still tend to carry an

53

affinity (resonance) with the cetaceans. They may also tend to feel more comfortable in a heavier body that is more similar to a cetacean form.

Also, many souls have had experiences within the angelic realm and tend to carry the angelic consciousness with them in their current human embodiment. Angelic consciousness is recognizable by its feeling of 'lightness,' and usually the body form tends to be slight or petite.

There are yet other possibilities. Throughout the many past experiences of souls, they may have chosen to experience life as a form within the nature kingdom, such as a tree deva or a mountain deva, or one of the many animal forms. In the celestial systems throughout our universe, a virtually infinite number of different body forms are available into which souls may incarnate. Some of these are more evolved versions of animal forms that are present here on Earth. If a soul has an extensive history of embodiments in one of these forms, such as a feline form for example, the human body in which they are currently embodied here on Earth may take on a feline appearance, especially in the facial features. If one's soul has a history in other than humanoid forms, it is not uncommon in the early moments of awakening from sleep to feel a bit strange coming back into a human body.

Soul transfers ('walk-ins')

Next, let's consider the subject of 'soul transfers,' more commonly known as 'walk-ins,' One of the early books on this subject, *Strangers Among Us*, was written by Ruth Montgomery in 1979.[6] A 'walk-in,' as she introduced the concept, is a situation in which the soul that has been associated with an embodiment since birth agrees to leave the body and make it available to be embodied by a different soul. There are various reasons why a soul might agree to do this. For example, it may involve a person that is very discouraged with life and no longer wants to live. So, rather than going through the death of the physical body, the original soul may make it available for another soul to embody. The 'incoming' soul has to agree to take on all of the 'karmic' responsibilities of that life, such as children (if there are any) or perhaps aging parents, and so on.

In every walk-in situation, an agreement must be made between the outgoing and incoming souls. However, since the agreements are made at the soul level, the human self may not be consciously aware that a soul transfer has been planned. Since the incoming soul inherits the memory within the body, in most cases the human self is not aware, at least initially, that a soul transfer has taken place.

In Ruth Montgomery's book, she indicated that an incoming soul is almost always a more evolved soul than the outgoing soul. This created an impression that if someone is a 'walk-in,' they must be a highly evolved person. It is true that a soul must be at a certainly level of evolutionary development before it is permitted to come in as a walk-in, and it is also true that many of the souls who came in as walk-ins during the 1970's and 1980's were highly evolved souls. But many of the souls who have come in as walk-ins during the past few decades have struggled to adapt to the human life situation they have entered. More than a few have become entangled in dysfunctional personality patterns inherited from the outgoing soul, and have allowed themselves to be diverted from their soul's mission and purpose.

Some misconceptions have been perpetuated about the circumstances under which the actual soul transfer takes place. The earlier perspectives were that the transfer almost always took place in conjunction with a traumatic situation, such as a car accident or severe illness. Although that seems to be true in some cases, many soul transfers take place rather seamlessly, without trauma involved. It is true, however, that trauma tends to shatter rigid energy patterns, sometimes making it easier for the incoming soul to integrate into the human form.

Although most soul transfers take place in mid-life, they occasionally take place during the first few years of life, or even in the senior years. Also, it is not uncommon for a person to undergo multiple walk-in experiences, separated by a few years, or in some cases many years.

The most noticeable and challenging issue for an incoming soul is that it quite likely will not have the same feelings of warmth or familiarity toward various family members or friends. As a result, many marriages do not survive very long after a soul transfer takes place.

At this point it might be helpful to share about my own experience. My first soul transfer (walk-in) took place in June, 1971, at 34 years of age. At that point in my life, I had no awareness of the concept of 'walk-

55

ins.' All I knew was that the focus of my life had shifted dramatically. I immersed myself in spiritual studies and practices, and became a vegetarian. It was not until several years later that I came upon Ruth Montgomery's book, and began to piece together what had happened to me.

In the period prior to the soul transfer, I had no feelings of deep depression or wanting to leave life, although in the preceding years, I had experienced the trauma of the death of my brother and the ending of my first marriage. At the time that the walk-in took place, I was remarried. But with the dramatic changes in my life, the marriage eventually ended, although we remained good friends. I continued my corporate career in the telecommunications industry, although my career was no longer the central focus in my life.

In 1992, I underwent a second walk-in experience. By this time, I was much more spiritually integrated, and having retired from my corporate career 3 years earlier, I was free to devote my full attention to my spiritual mission. My sense is that the soul/oversoul that came in during 1992 came to carry out a specific mission related to the completion of this planetary cycle.

My memory of my early life prior to the soul transfers is considerably diminished. I have vague recollections of various experiences, mostly the 'essence' of the experiences, but I remember very few specifics. Loss of detailed memory seems to be a common experience for many walk-ins.

As I reflect back over my life, I tend to view it in three segments, with each one having its own defining characteristics. My birth soul/oversoul was primarily focused on physical activity, whereas the soul/oversoul structure that 'walked in' during 1971 was more mentally oriented, with a deep interest in esoteric science. And finally, the soul/oversoul that entered through the walk-in process during 1992 is more heart-centered.

What are the advantages for a soul to enter as a walk-in rather than through the natural birth process? Assuming that the soul transfer takes place in mid-life, the incoming soul can focus on its mission and purpose much more quickly, without having to go through the stages of infancy and childhood. The primary risk of entering an embodiment as a walk-in is that it is all too easy to become encumbered by emotional and personality patterns that are already well established, patterns that may not be supportive to the life plan of the incoming soul.

Soul 'braiding'

Soul 'braiding' is a term used to describe a situation whereby a new soul merges into an existing embodiment, but the original birth soul does not leave. It is similar to the process described earlier in which more than one soul of an oversoul cluster join together in the same embodiment. Soul braiding, however, normally involves the merging in of a soul from a different oversoul cluster. In this sense, it becomes more like a 'hybrid' configuration.

Also, soul braiding tends to entail a more temporary situation, whereby a soul merges in for a period of time, and then later withdraws. For example, one case of which we are aware involved a soul who had never been embodied on Earth before. Before making a decision to embody for a full lifetime, this soul wanted to have a short 'trial' experience. So, with the permission of the 'host,' this soul merged in as a 'braid' for a few days to experience life through the body of the host.

Another example would be a situation in which a soul with special talents and abilities might want to come into an embodiment for a period of time to carry out a specific mission.

Entities ('uninvited guests')

Next, let's discuss a very different issue, but one that could easily be confused with a walk-in or soul braid.

When a soul completes a lifetime here on Earth, it is intended that the soul return to the higher realms and resume its evolutionary journey. However, in some cases a soul may be unwilling or unable to fully let go of the human experience just completed. This may be for a variety of different reasons. One of the more common reasons involves addictive behavioral patterns such as alcohol or drug abuse, gambling, or sexual addictions.

In such cases, when the soul leaves (through death) the body in which the addictive behavior developed, it remains attracted to places or situations in which people are involved in these activities, such as bars, gambling casinos, strip joints or bordellos. However, because the soul is no longer in a physical body, it can only *observe* other humans that are involved in these behaviors, it cannot experience the *feelings* of the addictive behaviors. The only way the soul can do that is to merge into the embodiment of someone who is involved in these behaviors and experience the feelings through that person's body. All too often in such cases, the wayward soul then becomes 'entrapped' in the body of the other person and does not know how to leave, or perhaps does not want to leave.

From the perspective of the person who has been invaded by the 'uninvited' soul, it is what is commonly referred to as being 'possessed,' or as having an 'entity' within the body. The best protection from being invaded by such a disembodied entity is to maintain a strong and healthy energy field, and of course, to avoid addictive behaviors. Unfortunately, drugs and alcohol severely *weaken* one's energy field, and make such a person especially vulnerable to intrusion.

Other circumstances also quite often attract entities. Most common are situations that involve 'emotional vulnerability.' An example would be a person who becomes distraught over the death of a family member or friend. Such a person might then attract a disembodied entity that would, with all good intentions, attempt to comfort them. If the entity is not careful, however, it can easily become entrapped in the body of the distraught person. It is not uncommon for such entrapments to continue on for many years, in some cases, a lifetime.

Having an attached entity is never a healthy situation, regardless of whether the original intent of the entity was for selfish pleasure or to be compassionately supportive. First and foremost, having an entity is always a drain on the energy supply of the body. Secondly, it can result in personality disorders. For example, if the attached entity has an abusive personality, it can at times overshadow the normal personality of the host. Thirdly, having an attached entity can create a severe distraction from the life plan of the person involved.

58

Experience has revealed that if a person has one attached entity, it is likely that they will have more than one. The more entities a person has, the greater the drain on their energy level. It is quite likely that many cases of Chronic Fatigue Syndrome involve attached entities. Another problem is that if a person has multiple entities, it can be very difficult for the host soul to 'find its own voice,' to function in life with clarity.

How does one know if a person has one or more attached entities? Inconsistency in personality characteristics is one of the most common indicators – sometimes pleasant, but at other times offensive or abusive. Also, people with attached entities invariably tend to avoid direct eye contact; the entities are in effect 'hiding' inside, and they are afraid that they might be seen. Indeed, they can be seen by a skilled spiritual counselor.

Unfortunately, because stories of 'demonic possession' have been the subject of numerous horror movies, a stigma tends to be associated with anyone who may, knowingly or unknowingly, have attached entities. The good news is that in recent years, this issue is becoming better understood, and an increasing number of spiritual counselors are available to assist in identifying and releasing entities.

Chapter 11

Interdimensional Communication

The term 'interdimensional communication' is being used to refer to communication that takes place between dimensional realities. In other words, this form of communication is achieved through other than the 5 senses of our physical reality. Three primary types of such communication are:

- 'Intuition' is essentially communication that takes place between our soul and our human self, as discussed in Chapter 4.
- 'Mind-to-mind' communication with beings in other realms, such as our guides and teachers, or people who have crossed over to the 'other side' through physical 'death.'
- Communication through 'consciousness,' such as accessing the consciousness of our Higher Self or the consciousness of the 'ALLNESS THAT IS.'

Let's explore each of the forms of communication in more depth.

Intuition

As our soul evolves from lifetime to lifetime, it retains the complete memory of all of our experiences, including our experiences between lifetimes. Our soul is also a repository for the wisdom that has accrued through these life experiences.

Although we presently know very little about the functional structure of our soul, it would be helpful to think of this cumulative memory and wisdom as being contained in our 'soul-mind.' Earlier in this book we discussed our 'heart-mind,' and indicated that it is associated with our 'heart-brain.' Intuition is communication that takes place between our soul-mind and our heart-mind.

Since the discovery of our heart-brain is quite recent, relatively little is known about the structure and functionality of this brain. Consequently, the mechanics of how intuition flows from our soul-mind to our heart-mind remains mostly a mystery at this time. However, as discussed earlier in this book, we can learn techniques for enhancing this intuitive flow.

Interdimensional mind-to-mind communication

Our crown chakra is our primary communication gateway to beings in other realms. This chakra functions in conjunction with the pineal gland, which is located in the center of our head, at the top of the brain stem.

A detailed explanation as to how communication is received through our crown chakra is provided in Appendix D. We believe that it is of interest to note that in contrast to intuition, which is focused in the area of our *heart*, communication through our crown chakra involves functional aspects of our brain and glandular systems that are located in our *head*.

Accessing consciousness

Consciousness is the 'language' of our Higher Self. It is beyond words, beyond thoughts. When we are able to access consciousness, it comes to us as 'knowingness.'

A discussion of the process through which consciousness may be accessed is provided in Appendix E.

As our spiritual awakening and transformation progresses, we gradually develop the ability to tune into and be receptive to the consciousness of our Higher Self – and ultimately to the consciousness of the 'ALLNESS THAT IS.' At that point, there is no consciousness anywhere in Creation that cannot be accessed. The consciousness of a tree or a bird, or even the consciousness of a rock is available to us. So also is the consciousness of a planet, a star, or an entire galaxy. Life then has the potential to become more expansive than we can possibly imagine.

Chapter 12

Interdimensional Healing

In Chapter 7, A Healthy Body, we discussed health issues and opportunities from a *human* perspective. In this chapter, our focus will be on healing and rejuvenation primarily from an *interdimensional* perspective.[7]

Support teams

Once we have achieved a degree of healing and cleansing within our physical, emotional, and mental bodies, we then have an opportunity to proceed with a more refined healing and purification process. This normally involves assistance from our 'support teams' within the higher dimensions.

As we previously indicated, before entering incarnation a 'life plan' is established to guide the course of our human life. As part of this life plan, we make agreements with other souls who will be significantly involved in our life. Such agreements may include 'support teams' within the higher dimensions that will be available to assist us with various aspects of our life. An important element of this assistance involves our healing and purification processes. Support teams typically include the following:

- Souls who have had experience in the medical and healing professions in various lifetimes often agree to provide assistance when they are 'in-between' lifetimes. In some situations they may assist us directly on an energetic level.

- Or in other cases, they may work through embodied medical and health professionals, guiding them as they work with us.

- Some angelic beings are especially adept at providing healing assistance to humans. This is a path of service that they have chosen. They work with us primarily on an energetic level.

- One of the most important groups of beings are the 'extraterrestrials' – beings from other star systems who are here in voluntary service to Earth. They function from within their spaceships, and in fact, some of their ships are designed especially for providing healing and rejuvenation support. They also have access to various 'healing centers' located throughout our galaxy and beyond.

An extremely important factor related to these support teams is the *'universal principle of non-interference,'* which restrains them from helping us unless we ask for their assistance. Our request for help can take many different forms. Sometimes we may want to ask for healing assistance related to a specific situation with which we are dealing, either physical or emotional in nature. But we are not always aware of health situations within our body that may need attention. Also, we are usually not fully aware of the capabilities of our support teams, especially the extraterrestrials. So in addition to specific requests, it is wise for us to put forth requests of a more general nature, such as asking for healing assistance for 'anything that would be in my highest good, and that would support my life's mission and purpose.'

There is another important consideration – that relates to ascension. Our preparation for ascension involves a significant amount of healing and purification within both our physical body and our energy body. Our support teams, especially the extraterrestrials, can be of great assistance in this regard.

Although innumerable processes and technologies can be employed, we will share a few examples from our own experience to provide a sense of some of the possibilities.

Spinning

A group of exercises, sometimes referred to as the 'Seven Sacred Rites,' has been in fairly widespread use among those seeking spiritual transformation. One of these seven rites involves extending the arms out to the sides from the shoulders, and then spinning around. This is very similar to a sacred dance of the Dervishes, for which they have become known as the 'Whirling Dervishes.'

The purpose of spinning is to help release toxins from the cellular structures of the physical body, and it seems to have a similar purifying effect on our energy body. Usually when one first begins to do the spinning exercise, there is a tendency to become dizzy or sometimes even nauseous after just a few revolutions. However, for those who have the fortitude to continue with the exercise over a period of time, the experience of dizziness and nausea gradually diminishes.

One of the purification procedures available on some spaceships is very similar to this. One stands on a small circular platform, which is then rotated. We normally undergo this experience in our higher dimensional body, not our physical body. Again, the purpose is to facilitate purification.

To share a personal story, my own first experience with this was not pleasant! It occurred in late 1991. One day in the late afternoon I suddenly became very sleepy, so I decided to take a short nap. When I awoke, a couple of hours had passed, and it felt like I had been in a very deep sleep. As I started to get up from the bed, I immediately became very dizzy and nauseous. I quickly laid back down on the bed, but the vertigo continued. Several subsequent attempts to get out of bed produced the same result. I finally decided to just stay in bed for the night, and was eventually able to go to sleep. When I awoke in the morning, most of the vertigo was gone. However, I continued to feel somewhat disoriented for the next couple of days.

At that time I had no memory of what had happened during my 'nap.' However, my guidance confirmed that my nausea and disorientation were the result of a process that I had undergone on a spaceship. During the next few months, the procedure was occasionally repeated. However, the vertigo and nausea were mild compared to the initial experience. Several months later, I was with a friend with whom I have shared many interdimensional experiences. While both taking a nap, were taken out to a ship (in our higher-dimensional bodies), and underwent the spinning process together. Fortunately, she is able to retain fairly complete memory of her other-dimensional experiences, so she was able to describe the process to me in considerable detail. We both continue to have experiences with the spinning process, sometimes together and sometimes individually, and we have become aware that others seem to have undergone similar experiences.

Clearing memory

It seems to be a fairly common experience among people who are progressing through their spiritual awakening and transformation processes that memory of earlier parts of their lives tends to diminish. This is especially true of walk-ins. Various factors may be involved in this, but we would like to share a particular perspective.

In a normal life cycle, we go through various experiences throughout the course of our life, and then very soon after our 'death,' we are led through a life review. In this process, we, along with our mentors, review each of the significant experiences of our life, to discover what can be learned. Through this process, the energetic intensity of the memory of each experience is released, leaving only a dim residual memory. Thus, at the completion of the review process, we are ready to begin the next phase of our evolutionary journey in the non-physical realms free of the encumbrance of intense past memories.

However, the life plan for this incarnation for many who are awakening spiritually anticipates that we will complete this incarnation through the ascension process, rather than going through physical 'death.' Thus, as an important part of our preparation for ascension, it is essential that we complete as much as possible of the 'life review' process prior to ascension. So occasionally, as we progress in our healing and purification process, we are taken to various places within the higher realms and are led through segments of this life review process. As various portions are completed, the energetic memories (both emotional and mental) are released, just as they would be in an after-death review process. From that point on, our ability to consciously access such memory is greatly diminished. In effect, this frees us up from the encumbrances of past human experiences, and enables us to more easily move forward with our emerging life.

A close friend had such an experience one night while we were staying at Mt. Shasta. She remembers being taken to a facility on the star system Sirius. While there, she was guided through a review of some of the male/female relationships that she had experienced early in her adult life. Similar to an 'after life' review, the purpose of this was to glean what could be learned from the experiences and then release them. Since that time, her memory and feelings related to those relationship experiences are greatly diminished. She was told at that time that the Siriuns are especially adept at this kind of work, and that many of us from Earth have traveled there to undergo such a review and release process.

Spiritual transformation involves letting go of old 'baggage' that is no longer relevant to our soul's mission and purpose.

Opening channels in our head

As we progress in our spiritual development, a considerable amount of work is done on us by our support teams. Some of this work involves opening various energy and communication channels in our head.

In many cases this work is done on our energy body while we are sleeping. Because of this, we may sometimes go to bed at night, or lay down for a nap feeling absolutely fine, but then awaken with discomfort in our head. My experience has been that such sensations do not last long, usually less than an hour.

Occasionally, I have had the experience of awakening prematurely, before the work is completed. In such a situation, somehow I intuitively *know* that I am not supposed to move yet. Even if my mind attempts to send signals to certain parts of my body to start moving, it is as though I simply don't have the 'will' to carry through with those movements. It is like being in some sort of a force-field that prevents me from moving until after the work is completed. I know others who have had similar experiences.

Summary

These are only a few examples of the types of assistance available to us related to our interdimensional healing and transformation process. A couple of important considerations to keep in mind are:

- If one feels disoriented or some discomfort immediately upon awakening, it is quite possible that some work has been done on us. Usually the disorientation does not last for more than a few minutes, or a few hours at most, but it is wise to be gentle with one's self.
- Most medical doctors are not aware that such interdimensional intervention is possible. If one goes to a doctor for assistance related to such experiences, there is a danger that symptoms will be misinterpreted, possibly resulting in inappropriate treatment being administered.

Although in our humanness we may sometimes feel that we have lost control of our transformational and healing processes, it is well to remember that in our requests for assistance and our surrender to the 'highest good,' we have invited and given consent for such intervention.

Part III

A Planetary Perspective

Chapter 13

History of Earth

The planning for Earth began long, long ago; some sources say that it began even before our Milky Way galaxy came into being. The primary goal that the designers of Earth had in mind was to create a planet of exquisite beauty, beauty that is unparalleled anywhere in the Universe. Among other aspects of the design, this involved seeding Earth with a wide variety of plants, animals and minerals. So as the planet was being formed, samples of life-forms were gathered from throughout our universe and brought here to Earth.

In the beginning

The cycle of evolution that will complete in the year 2012 began about 200,000 years ago. At least that was the time period in which a life wave of souls was seeded in human form here on Earth. In the beginning these souls retained awareness of their Divine nature, their inherent connection to their Creator. So it was only natural that the emerging civilization was based on love, compassion, and a respect for all life. Because of the natural beauty of Earth, life in those days was idyllic – hence the Biblical reference to the 'Garden of Eden.'

The 'laggard' souls

However, partway through this cycle, a planet elsewhere in our universe with a very different civilization began to experience problems. Most of the inhabitants of that planet lived lives based on 'service to self'

73

rather than consideration for the good of all. They were technologically advanced, but much of their technology was directed toward the development of weaponry for use in their ongoing wars. The weapons had become so destructive that their planet was becoming uninhabitable. So the overseers of the planet sent out a plea for help.

Those of the spiritual hierarchy who were responsible for Earth were approached with a request to accept the beings from this imperiled planet into the civilization on Earth. It was hoped that by living within such a gentle and loving situation, the ego-centered souls from the warring planet would soon see the wisdom of a more peaceful way of life. A decision had to be made fairly quickly because the demise of their planet was imminent. Although the spiritual council responsible for Earth was apprehensive, they decided to acquiesce to the request.

So, a plan was carefully developed. It included many precautions, such as teaching these souls about the ways of Earth before they were brought here. They arrived during the mid-point of the Lemurian civilization. In the early stages, all seemed to be going well. These souls were grateful for having been rescued, and they found it easy to merge into the gentle and compassionate civilization on Earth. Unfortunately, it was not long before they began to fall back into their old ways of greed and violence, and in doing so, gradually contaminated some of the souls of Earth. Some sources refer to the souls who came to Earth from the warring planet as the 'laggards,' because they were lagging behind in their evolutionary progress.[8]

Inner Earth beings

Over a period of time, some of the original souls of Earth retreated to remote areas of the planet so they could minimize their involvement with the laggards. A sizeable group of the original souls of Earth decided to shift their bodies to a higher frequency, an ability that they still retained, and dwell *within* the Earth, rather than on the surface. Those souls have retained their higher consciousness, and the plan is that they will emerge and reconnect with the surface civilization at the end of this cycle. In fact, the early stages of this seem to have already begun. There are 'portals' into inner Earth at certain locations on our planet. Mt. Shasta, in northern California, is one of these locations, and several books have been written about the underground city of Telos, including contacts with some of the inhabitants. More recently, in an interview by Lilou Mace, Drunvalo Melchizedek described some of his interactions with inner-Earth beings who travel in and out of Earth through a portal in Mexico.[9]

Duality – the experiment

Eons ago yet another experiment was initiated here on Earth. The beings who had responsibility for Earth were curious as to what would happen if the souls, as they entered into human embodiment, were 'veiled' from their conscious awareness of their connection to their Creator, their Oneness with Source. Would it provide an important learning experience for these souls to experience life in the illusion of 'separateness' from Source and from each other? And, through the experience of 'separateness,' would they gain a deeper understanding and appreciation of the nature of Oneness? Thus began the experiment in 'duality.'

Off-planet beings of malevolent intent

The history of Earth involves yet another layer of complexity. Over time, beings of 'misguided intent' from off-planet realms developed linkages with the laggard souls on Earth. Some of these beings presented themselves as 'gods,' and proceeded to exert control over humanity for their own selfish purposes. Human DNA was manipulated to 'dumb down' humans, making them easier to control. This has added immeasurably to the suppression of evolutionary progress within our world. It was primarily this intrusion of off-planet beings, functioning in alliance with the laggard souls, that developed perverted technology in the latter stages of Atlantis. As we know, this eventually brought about the demise of Atlantis and plunged the civilization of Earth deeper into density. And so the struggle continues. As Winston Churchill once observed, "The history of Earth is just one damn thing after another!"

The grand design

As discussed briefly in the Introduction of this book, the grand design of the cosmos provides that as universes, galaxies, star systems, and planets evolve, they become less and less dense. In other words, they vibrate at a higher frequency. But evolutionary progression must proceed in a synchronized manner. In the aftermath of the fall of Atlantis, Earth plunged deeper and deeper into density. It is said to currently be the densest planet within our universe that is inhabited by sentient beings. And it is holding back the evolutionary progress of our entire universe. This is why the 'ascension' of Earth to a higher dimension (higher frequency) is absolutely essential as we complete this long cycle of evolution in 2012.

The 'Lightworkers'

As the council of beings within the spiritual realms that has responsibility for the evolution of Earth monitored the situation, it was becoming evident that some form of intervention was needed to uplift the civilization of Earth. So a plan was devised to bring a group of highly evolved souls to Earth to incarnate in human form, and to provide leadership and inspiration for the development of a more enlightened civilization. The first group consisted of 144,000, and was under the leadership of Lord Melchizedek. They came to Earth in approximately 4,000 BC, about the beginning of recorded history on our planet. They tended to incarnate in groups at specific locations on the planet. The enlightened civilizations of ancient Egypt, Greece, and other times and places can be attributed to this group of beings.

Throughout the intervening centuries, and especially in recent times, many, many additional highly evolved souls from other celestial worlds have come to Earth to assist. Some have incarnated in human form, some in cetacean forms (whales and dolphins), and many serve on the spaceships surrounding Earth, providing support from that realm. Virtually all of these souls, including the original group, agreed to remain with Earth until the end of this evolutionary cycle in 2012.

The Continuing Struggle

The dawning of the 20th century saw our planet plunge even deeper into the dark abyss. With two world wars and the associated human atrocities, the future of Earth was becoming increasingly uncertain. This reached a crisis point with the development and detonation of atomic weapons during the 1940's.

Intervention

The principle of 'free will' is fundamental to the evolutionary scheme in our universe. However, it was becoming increasingly apparent that if the beings of Earth continued on the course they were on at that time, they most likely would destroy the planet through the use of nuclear weapons that were being developed at an accelerated pace. And of equally great concern, the destruction of Earth would inevitably cause severe damage to the entire galactic 'neighborhood.'

So, at this point, the Creator of our universe issued a decree that nuclear weapons would not be permitted to be used as weapons of war on planet Earth. Nor would they be allowed to be sent out into space. Responsibility for carrying out this decree was assigned primarily to the Intergalactic Federation. This will be discussed in more detail later in the book.

By the end of World War II, less than 7 decades remained in our current evolutionary cycle. Once again, planning within the higher spiritual realms was taking on an escalating sense of urgency. Without a major thrust, it was not likely that Earth could be ready for ascension by the end of the cycle in 2012.

So plans were made for a new influx of Lightworkers into the planetary realm. This wave of assistance included many of the original 144,000, as well as evolved beings from throughout our galaxy and beyond. A large number of these came into embodiment through the natural birth process during the last half of the 1940's and the early part of the 1950's. A second phase of this wave came into embodiment through the 'walk-in' process during the late 1960's and throughout the 1970's and early 1980's.

Chapter 14

The 'New Earth'

The efforts of the Lightworkers were being supported with infusions of transformational energies directed to Earth from celestial sources. By the mid-1970's, it was becoming evident that substantial progress was being made in the collaborative efforts to awaken the consciousness of humanity and raise the vibrations of our planet. But it was equally apparent that Earth still had a very long way to go before it would be ready for ascension to a higher dimension. The end of the evolutionary cycle was fast approaching, less than 40 years in the future. That is a substantial period of time relative to a human life span, but a mere 'blink of an eye' in the context of planetary evolution.

It was time for a new plan. Because of the progress that had been made in shifting the consciousness of humanity, the Creator of our universe once again intervened. A decree was issued that had two separate but related elements:

- A 'New Earth' would be created. It would be a pristine version of the original Earth, in all of its beauty, purity and perfection. It would ultimately reside within the 5th dimension.
- All conscious beings on Earth would be assured an opportunity to ascend to the 'New Earth' within the 5th dimension, so long as they make the choice to do so and complete the necessary preparation for the ascension process. (The steps involved in preparing for ascension will be discussed later.)

So the creation of the New Earth began. This approach to ascension is unique within our universe, it has never been done this way before, and that is one of the reasons that so many beings are here in spaceships surrounding our planet observing the process.

Planetary 'mitosis'?

The cosmic science involved in creating the New Earth is quite complex. An analogy would be the process that a human cell goes through when it splits into two cells, the process of 'mitosis.'

A long-time mentor of mine, Dr. Derald Langham, who was a plant geneticist, once described to me the process he observed through a microscope as he watched a cell split into two cells. Initially there is just one cell, and as mitosis begins, the new cell that is in formation occupies the same space as the original cell. Over a period of time, slight movements are observable as the new cell is being formed. Gradually, the movements become more pronounced and more rapid. The process seems to have some of the same characteristics as sexual orgasm. At the culmination point, the new cell splits off from the original cell. From then on, they exist as two separate cells.

In a similar manner, the New Earth that is in the process of formation, currently occupies the same 'space' as the original Earth. However, a new 'Light-grid' has been formed, and the New Earth is coalescing around the framework of this new grid.

Consciousness of the New Earth

For those of us who have chosen the path of ascension, it is essential that we align our self, and all aspects of our life, with the consciousness of the New Earth. Yes, we are still able to observe that which is associated with the 'Old Earth.' The television news channels continue to be, for the most part, linked into the consciousness of the Old Earth. Also, as we go about our daily lives, we certainly encounter human behavioral patterns that are expressions of the consciousness of the Old Earth. But the more we are able to maintain an alignment with the consciousness of the New Earth, the more we accelerate our preparation for ascension, and the more we assist in bringing the new planet into manifestation.

The key to aligning our self with the consciousness of the New Earth involves our heart, maintaining an alignment with the love and wisdom that resides within our heart, as discussed earlier in this book.

The Residual Earth (Old Earth)

It is not clear at this time what the future of the 'residual' 3rd dimensional Earth (Old Earth) will be. Those souls who have chosen to remain at the 3rd dimensional level as we move into the next evolutionary cycle most likely will remain on the Old Earth for a period of time after the two versions of Earth split. But this probably will only be a transitional situation. In the long term, the 3rd dimensional version of Earth is being 'phased out,' and the souls who have chosen to continue their evolutionary journey within the 3rd dimension will most likely be relocated to other 3rd dimensional worlds. It is not clear, however, how this transition will be accomplished, or whether the transition period will be a matter of days, months, years, or lifetimes.

Chapter 15

Indigo, Crystal & Rainbow Children

In conjunction with the decree by our Creator that nothing would be permitted to interfere with the ascension process at the end of this evolutionary cycle, a decision was made within the spiritual hierarchy to infuse humanity on Earth with yet another large group of highly advanced souls. These souls would incarnate throughout the world with the specific purpose of instigating needed changes in virtually every aspect of human civilization. These souls eventually became known as the 'Indigo Children.' Subsequent incoming waves of these advanced souls have become known as the 'Crystal Children' and 'Rainbow Children.'

The intent was that these souls would help to further awaken the consciousness of humanity on Earth and bring about as much change as possible in preparation for ascension. Then as they moved through ascension to the New Earth, they would form the foundation of the emerging civilization on the New Earth. From the perspective of those of us living on Earth when these advanced souls began to arrive, the entry of these souls into our planetary civilization unfolded essentially as follows.

Beginning in the late 1970's and throughout the 1980's, spiritually-aware people began to notice that some of the young children seemed to be unusually sensitive and psychically gifted.

In 1982, Nancy Ann Tappe authored a book entitled *Understanding Your Life Through Color*.[10] One of the color categories she discussed in the book was 'Indigo,' and she noticed that many of the characteristics inherent in these new children seemed to fit the characteristics associated with the Indigo category. Nancy is also able to see people's auras, and she noticed that most of these children had a lot of indigo color in their auras. Consequently, thanks to Nancy's pioneering work, these children soon became known as the 'Indigo Children.'

In that timeframe, however, not many people were paying much attention to these gifted children. But as they began to enter school and progress through our educational systems, teachers and parents alike began to realize that many of these children were indeed *very* 'different' from other children.

We shall discuss some of these differences in a moment, but for now, let's continue on with the chronology. In the early 1990's, another wave of children began to emerge which have since been referred to as the 'Crystal Children.' And finally, since the beginning of the new century, a third wave of these special children is emerging; these have become known as the 'Rainbow Children.'

As indicated earlier, all of these advanced souls have been coming in at this time to participate in this final phase of the evolutionary cycle that is completing, and to be in a position to take on leadership roles within the spiritually-awakened civilization that will emerge on the New Earth.

During the past two decades, interest in the Indigo, Crystal and Rainbow Children has expanded dramatically. Many new books are now available, and numerous conferences have been held to share information and experiences, especially among parents and educators. Doreen Virtue has made a very helpful contribution to this educational endeavor, and her audio CD set entitled "Indigo, Crystal, and Rainbow Children" provides an excellent overview.[11]

Similarities among these young people

Although some differences distinguish the three groups – Indigo, Crystal and Rainbow – there are more similarities than differences. Following are some of the characteristic that are generally common to the three groups.

❖ Strong sense of self

They come in with a strong sense of self-worth – an awareness of who they are and the purpose for which they came into life. They expect to be treated with respect and to be reasoned with as though they were adults. They do not respond well to rules established by parents or teachers unless the reason and purpose for the rules are well understood – and they prefer to participate in working out the terms of such rules. They find physical punishment, such as spanking or being treated with physical roughness, to be especially abhorrent.

❖ Intuitive and telepathic

They tend to be able to read people's thoughts, so they usually know whether or not the words people are speaking are in alignment with what they are actually thinking. Also, they are either attracted to people or repelled by people, depending on what they sense in a person's heart.

❖ Clairvoyant and clairaudient

Many of these children are able to see into non-physical dimensions. It is not at all uncommon for them to have friends such as angels or other non-physical beings with whom they regularly converse. Many are also able to see people's auras, and sense whether the energy is light and uplifting, or dark and unpleasant. Some are also able to see energy forms, and naturally avoid going near places that are occupied by discordant energies.

❖ Sensitive to color and textures

Most are sensitive to color and textures, and have definite 'likes' and 'dislikes.' Many like to pick out their own clothing, even at a very early age. The color of rooms is important to them, and they sometimes have difficulty sleeping or relaxing in a room with 'loud' or gaudy colors.

❖ Sensitive to chemicals

Some of these gifted children are extremely sensitive to chemicals such as food additives, medications, or toxic environments. Food allergies can sometimes be a problem. Many of them are natural vegetarians.

❖ Past lives and other states of consciousness

It is quite common for these children to remember some of their past lives or experiences in non-physical realms between lifetimes. They also might remember embodiments in other than human forms. Some are occasionally able to remember experiences they have had in other realms while their body is sleeping.

❖ Seek friendships with other 'aware' children

As these children move through their developmental years and begin to progress through the school systems, many have come to realize that most adults, often including their parents and teachers, 'just don't get it.' So they gradually become much more cautious in talking about their experiences. The tendency is for them to seek friendships among contemporaries who can more easily relate to their feelings and experiences.

Let's now consider some of the characteristics that are unique to each of the three groups.

Indigo children

The primary mission of the Indigos is to serve as *agents of change*:
- from competition to cooperation
- from greed to sharing and compassion
- from violence to peaceful mediation
- from abuse of our planet to respect and caring

- from deceit and corruption to integrity
- from prejudice to appreciation of diversity

Yes, it is a monumental task that they have taken on! They have sometimes been referred to as 'systems busters' because they have come in to change the distorted and oftentimes corrupted institutions and cultural structures, rather than capitulate. Whereas other Lightworkers might tend to simply ignore the aspects of life with which they do not resonate, it is more difficult for the Indigos to disassociate. In this sense, they are like 'sacred warriors,' confronting rather than accommodating.

As a group, they have a tendency to be angry at earlier generations for the mess we have made of things. So dealing with anger is definitely one of the challenges for many of the Indigos.[12] Understandably, Indigo children generally do not hesitate to question and challenge adult authority when it is not based on integrity.

Indigos tend to be either right-brain dominant or at least balanced between right-brain and left-brain dominance. This puts them at odds with our current educational systems which over-emphasize left-brain achievement. Since these right-brain Indigos tend to learn more easily through unstructured activities and movement, being forced to sit quietly at a desk for long periods of time is a direct confrontation to their natural learning rhythms. Consequently, many of the Indigo children have been incorrectly diagnosed as having Attention Deficit Disorder (ADD) or Attention Deficit Hyperactivity Disorder (ADHD) issues. Unfortunately, far too many medical practitioners have tended to prescribe medications which almost always exacerbate the situation.

The main wave of advanced souls who came in as the Indigo children are now in their twenties. Those on the leading edge of the wave are in their thirties, while those at the trailing edge of the wave are in their teens.

As previously indicated, their role is to *bring about change on our planet*. The Indigo children of yesteryear have become the young 'activists' of today. An important focus for many of these activists has been the environment, many getting their start through school projects and youth organizations, and later working through existing environmental organizations or creating new ones.

In his 2007 book, *Blessed Unrest*, Paul Hawken writes:

> "The dawn of the twenty-first century has witnessed two remarkable developments in our history: the appearance of systemic problems that are genuinely global in scope, and the growth of a worldwide movement that is determined to heal the wounds of the earth with the force of passion, dedication, and collective intelligence and wisdom. Across the planet groups ranging from ad hoc neighborhood associations to well-funded international organizations are confronting issues like the destruction of the environment, the abuse of free-market fundamentalism, social justice, and the loss of indigenous cultures." [13]

The Indigo activists are making their presence felt in virtually every country of the world. At the time of this writing, the revolution that began in Tunisia has toppled the old Mubarak regime in Egypt, and revolution has spread to Libya, Syria, and several other countries throughout the Middle-East. We can safely assume that many Indigo activists are playing key roles, and will continue to be deeply involved in the transformation that is unfolding.

We are only in the very early stages of changes to take place throughout the world – changes in governments, yes, but also in corporations, financial systems, religious organizations, medical and pharmaceutical conglomerates, 'factory farms' and giant food monopolies, the petro-chemical cartels – the list is seemingly endless.

John F. Kennedy once said, "Those who make peaceful revolution impossible will make violent revolution inevitable." Let's hope that most of the changes that are needed on our planet can be brought about in non-violent ways.

Crystal children

These children come in on a vibration of pure LOVE. Quite naturally they tend to judge people based on whether or not they have open hearts. One way to recognize the Crystal children is that they tend to have large eyes that feel like they are looking into the depth of your soul when they look at you.

Compared to Indigo children, Crystal children tend to be much easier to raise. For one reason, they tend not to have issues with anger in the way that the Indigos do. In fact they tend to be quite affectionate, and love to hug. The Crystal children also tend to be very compassionate, and naturally respond toward people who are in need. Many of them also seem to be drawn to elderly people, and easily develop loving relationships with them.

The Crystals seem to have a very close relationship with nature, especially with animals. They love to be outdoors and seem to have a special appreciation for the beauty of Earth. For example, some of the Crystal kids have been known to get very upset when someone picks flowers to make a bouquet, since they would much prefer to see the flowers continue living in their natural setting.

Many of the Crystal children seem to have a natural ability to communicate with plants and animals. And not surprisingly, many of these children seem to be natural vegetarians.

Because Crystal children tend to be very telepathic, it is not uncommon for them to talk very little until they are 3 or 4 years old. In some cases this has been misdiagnosed as Autism.

Rainbow children

Because the Rainbow children have started arriving here on Earth much more recently, not as much is known about them. They get their name from the fact that they seem to love color, and are very discerning regarding subtle differences in hues. They also seem to be highly creative.

Their personalities have been noted to be very dolphin-like, with a natural joy and playfulness. However, they also have very strong wills and personalities. For many of them, this is their first time on Earth, and they seem to be fearless and trusting of everyone.

Dawn of tomorrow

The role of the Crystal and Rainbow children will be to assist in laying the foundations of a new civilization. They carry within their essence the vibrations of Love and Joy, and these will be the keynotes of our new world. Their love for nature will help to restore respect for the beauty of Earth. And their open hearts will enable a trusting relationship with all of the animals of our planet as well as a renewed appreciation and respect for all life forms.

Chapter 16

Our Reality is Shifting

The reality that we perceive through our senses is shifting. The 'veils,' or barriers between dimensions, are becoming more transparent. As the awakening of consciousness accelerates, and the energetic frequencies of our human reality continue to increase, a growing number of people around the world are finding that they are having experiences that are not explainable within the framework of our normal reality.

Some people are occasionally having a sense of being in two different realities at the same time. Or sometimes a sense of reality that seemed quite 'normal' only moments ago, suddenly shifts, and we find our self in a reality that feels quite 'different.' It often is hard to find words to describe the shift that we have experienced, somehow it just 'feels different.' Such altered states of reality seem to be confusing for some people, while others find them uplifting, as though they have somehow transcended into a world that is more joyful and inspiring.

Oftentimes these experiences are accompanied by a sense that 'time' is accelerating, or becoming much more 'fluid.' For example, we may get up in the morning and go about our day, and about the time our senses tell us that it must be mid-morning, we look at a clock and find it is almost noon already. Likewise the days of the week seem to come and go much faster.

Various phenomena are also showing up in our human reality that are not explainable from a conventional perspective. Let's consider a few examples.

Orbs

With the emergence of digital photography, people began to notice that occasionally small circular 'blotches' of light would show up in the pictures they had taken. Initially most people would try to explain them away as some sort of reflections caused by the lens. But gradually it became apparent that the appearance of these circles of light, or 'Orbs' as they have come to be known, was something more than a random phenomenon.

For example, they seemed to show up more often in pictures of people who were having a good time. Also, groups of people who were gathered around a spiritual focus, especially when it involved uplifting music, seemed to attract Orbs.

As interest in Orbs grew, people started experimenting in order to learn more about them. Many found that if they invited the Orbs to be present and show up in a picture, the Orbs tended to respond to the invitation, occasionally in large numbers. This seemed to indicate that Orbs must be some form of conscious beings.

Also, as the quality of digital cameras improved so that pictures were of higher resolution, the intricate 'mandala-like' patterns and colors of the Orbs became apparent.

Gradually, an increasing number of people have begun to sense when Orbs are present, and in some cases to actually see them in their vision. At this point, it is not clear whether the 'seeing' is an expanded spectrum seen with the physical eyes, or if the Orbs are being seen with inner vision through the third eye.

Crop circles

Virtually all of us are aware of 'crop circles.' These are geometric patterns that began showing up in grain fields in the 1970's. The number and complexity of these crop circles have increased year by year. Although reports of them have come from 26 different countries, approximately 90% of them have shown up in southern England. Of these, about half have been within a 15 km radius of Avebury.

When the crop circles first began to appear, efforts were made by skeptics to debunk them as the work of pranksters. But as the complexity of these precise patterns has increased, it has become more difficult for any rational person to deny that the origin of these geometric patterns is not of our world. On a few occasions, spaceships have been observed at night in particular locations where crop circles have appeared the following morning.

Throughout the years numerous people have come up with plausible interpretations of the various geometric patterns involved, translating them into messages for the people of Earth. Most likely, however, it will not be until we have open contact with the extraterrestrials that we will have a full understanding of the origin and the messages contained within these beautiful and intricate patterns.

Spaceship clouds

Spaceships operating in the environs of Earth are generally required to maintain 'invisibility' so that they do not alarm the residents of Earth. Invisibility can be achieved either by operating within a dimension higher than the physical dimension of Earth, such as within the 4th or 5th dimension, or they can use a form of 'cloaking' which makes them invisible to human sight.

Under certain weather and atmospheric conditions, however, the energy field created by a ship precipitates a cloud of moisture particles around the ship in the same shape of the ship, which is visible to the human eye. Sometimes these cloud forms are clearly visible and obvious, while at other times they are more subtle. Most people don't notice them, especially if they are in denial that spaceships even exist. But once a person becomes accustomed to seeing them in the sky, it is difficult *not* to see them.

Such spaceship clouds are most commonly seen above mountains or mountain ranges. This is because the crust of the Earth tends to be more substantial in such areas, and it is safer for the ships to come in closer to the Earth without the danger of destabilizing the surface of the Earth with the force-field of the ship. Mt. Rainier, near Seattle, and Mt. Shasta, in northern California are areas where spaceship clouds are frequently observed.

The shape of spaceship clouds is most commonly in the form of a disk. Quite often the clouds (ships) are 'stacked' one on top of another, somewhat like a dish of pancakes. The larger ships are often of an elongated shape. Under certain atmospheric conditions, the smaller spaceship clouds disappear and reappear in a different location in a matter of a few minutes if the ships move from one place to another.

As the number of spaceships operating in the vicinity of Earth has increased in recent years, the regularity of spaceship clouds appearing in the sky has also increased dramatically. However, spaceship clouds have been appearing, at least in limited numbers, for many decades. One of the most famous photographs taken by the nature photographer, Ansel Adams, is called "Moonrise Hernandez." It was taken in 1941, looking toward the community of Hernandez, New Mexico, with the Sangre de Cristo Mountains in the background. Numerous spaceship clouds are clearly visible over the mountains in this photograph.

Animals: Inter-species friendships

During the past few years, an increasing number of videos depicting loving relationships between animals of different species have found their way onto the internet. In many cases these have been between animals of species that would normally have a predator/prey relationship toward each other. For example, in some cases the friendship has been between a cat and a bird, or a cat and a mouse. In other situations, the friendship has been between a deer and a dog, or a rabbit and a dog.

Some of the most unexpected situations involve close loving relationships between a human and a lion or a human and a tiger. One particular video shows a relationship between a man and a lioness, it shows them playing together, sometimes cuddling together just as though the lion was an overgrown domestic cat. The video also shows the lioness allowing the man to play with her baby cubs, seeming to appreciate the care and attention he is directing to her babies.

There have also been situations in which a nursing mother of one species has been seen regularly nursing an orphaned infant of another

94

species along with her own babies. Such an example of compassion seems to demonstrate that maternal instincts extend across arbitrary boundaries between species.

Many of the close, trusting relationships between humans and various animals derive from situations in which a very young animal has lost its mother, and a human has stepped in and cared for it as it grows from infancy to maturity.

At least a few exceptional situations involving loving inter-species friendships have probably always existed, but they seem to be occurring with much greater frequency. It is as though the consciousness of animals is awakening, and they are becoming more heart-centered, more loving and caring. It may be that animals are showing us humans the way to relationships of the future.

Such a shift in consciousness brings to mind the often quoted phrase from the Bible: "and the lion shall lay down with the lamb." The quote is actually an abbreviated version of the essence of a series of verses in Isaiah having to do with the transforming power of spirit.

Angels

Angels have played an important role throughout human history. Many religious texts refer to them regularly. In that context, angels seem to have come forth at crucial times to announce imminent events of great importance.

In contemporary times, angelic beings are sometimes observed at the scene of a catastrophic event, such as an airplane crash or automobile accident. Sometimes they are not seen at the time of the event, but later show up in photographs taken at the scene.

Also, just as the energy field of spaceships sometimes create 'clouds' that are the same shape of the ships and clearly visible, the energy fields of angelic beings in the sky also frequently precipitate a visible cloud around them. Similar to the spaceship clouds, once one becomes accustomed to seeing the 'angel clouds,' it soon becomes difficult *not* to see them or sense the energy emanating from them.

Each one of us has a 'guardian angel' who watches over us and protects us throughout our life. Again, with the awakening of

95

consciousness, many people are becoming more aware of their guardian angels and learning to interact with them more consciously. Many of us are learning to call on the angelic realms for assistance in our daily lives. And as we do, and as the veils continue to lift, an increasing number of people are able to 'see,' or at least 'sense,' the presence of angelic beings.

Part IV
Becoming a Galactic Human

Chapter 17

A Vision of Life on the New Earth

The path of ascension is the passageway to becoming a 'galactic human.' We came here to Earth from the stars, and we are in the process of returning to the stars. It is time to rejoin our 'galactic family.'

Our lives will change dramatically as we move through the ascension process and find ourselves in the 5th dimensional realm of the New Earth. In this chapter, it is our intent to provide a vision as to what our lives may be like as we co-create a new civilization on the New Earth.

The end of separateness

When we agreed to participate in the experiment involving 'duality,' we agreed to enter into human embodiment with intentional 'forgetfulness' of our Oneness with our Creator and with all of Creation. This included forgetfulness of our galactic family and the vast number of life experiences we have shared with them throughout our soul's celestial history.

Duality does not exist above the 4th dimension, so as we ascend to the 5th dimension, we will leave duality behind us forever! This means that we will live in full awareness of who we truly are, our Oneness with our Creator and with all of Creation. And we will recognize everyone else in the fullness of who they truly are.

We will have full memory of our 'past lives' on Earth, and also memory of the experiences we have had in other star systems throughout our long cosmic history. We will also reconnect with the beings of Inner Earth, those of our soul family from long ago that migrated to realms within the Earth in order to insulate themselves from the negativity that had permeated the civilization on the surface of our planet. What an incredible 'family reunion' this will be!

In Kahlil Gibran's book, *The Prophet*, he writes some interesting words near the end that seem to speak allegorically to our emergence from the experience of 'duality.'

> *"The veil that clouds your eyes shall be lifted by the hands that wove it,*
>
> *And the clay that fills your ears shall be pierced by those fingers that kneaded it.*
>
> *And you shall see.*
>
> *And you shall hear.*
>
> *Yet you shall not deplore having known blindness, nor regret having been deaf.*
>
> *For in that day you shall know the hidden purposes in all things,*
>
> *And you shall bless the darkness as you would bless the light."*

Health and wellbeing

Although we will take our physical bodies with us, the nature of our bodies after ascension will be very different. They will not be subject to illnesses, so the pervasive health issues that so many people experience in our current world will be only a dim memory from the past. We will enjoy the benefits of a body that retains perfect health and vitality, and does not age or die. As a special bonus for those of us who are in our 'senior' years here on Earth, we will have the opportunity to go through an age regression process that enables us to choose the age-related appearance of our body!

Restoration of our DNA

In Chapter 13 we indicated that long ago the DNA of our human bodies was partially deactivated by beings of malevolent intent in order to severely limit the functionality of our bodies, thus making humans much easier to control. The ascension process will restore our DNA to its fullness, thus dramatically increasing the capabilities of our human mind and body.

Enlightened social structures

As we reconnect on the New Earth with those with whom we have shared close and loving experiences in past lives, such as family members or close friends, the nature of our new social structures will most likely be much more 'inclusive' and 'expansive' than the structures to which we have become accustomed in our current world. As spiritual beings, it is normal and natural that we feel deep love for virtually everyone. This is especially true related to our feelings for those of our cosmic soul families with whom we have shared the evolutionary journey throughout eons of time.

Consciousness of the inhabitants of the New Earth

Earlier in the book we indicated that as planetary systems evolve, they correspondingly increase in frequency. The same is .true for individual souls. So frequency is an indicator of the level of evolvement of a soul. The progress of our evolvement in any particular lifetime is related to the degree to which we are able to integrate the virtues of our Creator into our consciousness (See Chapter 8). In other words, living our life with an open heart, and incorporating love and compassion into every aspect of our daily experiences is the way that we raise the frequency at which our soul functions.

Normally when a soul 'ascends' from a 3rd dimensional planet, it would ascend just one dimensional level, to a 4th dimensional world. In our present situation, however, souls that ascend to the New Earth will be going from a 3rd dimensional level to a 5th dimensional level. We would not be able to withstand such a 'double-level' ascension unless we are already functioning at a sufficiently high frequency. Consequently, 'frequency' will be the primary criterion that determines whether or not a person who is currently embodied on Earth will be able to pass through ascension to the New Earth.

The obvious implication of this is that the inhabitants of the New Earth will be only those beings who are of sufficiently evolved consciousness. So most of the problems that we have had to deal with on our 3rd dimensional Earth – greed, corruption, abusiveness, poverty, crime, war, intolerance – will not be present on the New Earth. Consequently, it will be only natural for the new civilization to focus on that which is in the highest good for all, with deep love and respect for our new planet. No one will lack the basic necessities of life, and all will have an opportunity to live joyful, meaningful and creative lives.

Children of the New Earth

As indicated earlier, the choice involving ascension is a choice that is made by each individual soul. Because of its crucial importance related to the future evolutionary path of each soul, the choice transcends consideration of current family structures. This implies that one or more child of a family may, on a soul level, choose the ascension path even if one or both parents do not. Therefore, one of the immediate needs on the New Earth will be to provide facilities and supportive social structures for children who arrive on the New Earth without parents. Planning and preparation for this is receiving careful attention within the higher realms.

Direct manifestation

We will be able to manifest most of the things we desire directly from Source, so there will be much less need for factories, with their inevitable environmental issues and necessity for manual laborers to perform monotonous, routine tasks. Also, we will be able to 'un-manifest' things we no longer need, returning them to primal substance. So the accumulation of 'garbage' will be a non-issue.

Also, because of our ability to directly manifest that which we desire, economic systems will not be required, at least not in the context of the economic system with which we are currently familiar. No rent or mortgage payments to deal with!

New technology

Many different forms of new technology will be provided to us by our galactic friends, making our lives less burdensome and more fulfilling. This will be especially helpful in the area of free energy sources and transportation systems that do not disfigure the landscape of our planet. Also, advanced robotic technology will make possible a society in which most mundane tasks are performed by androids.

Education and research

A major thrust within our civilization on the New Earth will involve education and research. This will be especially true for young people. Students will be able to learn in facilities that incorporate pleasant natural interior landscaping, and which utilize revolutionary new teaching/learning techniques.

Our educational and research systems, both for young people and adults, will most likely utilize significant numbers of guest educators from other star systems, thus greatly accelerating our progress in virtually all of the arts and sciences.

Performing arts

Many of the celestial worlds are highly advanced in the performing arts. Early in our experiences on the New Earth we most likely will be the beneficiaries of guest performances by some of these celestial performers.

Interstellar travel

Many of us here on Earth have found that traveling to various countries and interacting with a diversity of cultures have provided us some of our richest experiences. We can only imagine the splendor and fascination of the adventures that are in store for us as we travel to other star systems.

But interplanetary tourism will also involve beings from other planetary systems coming to the New Earth to become acquainted with us, and to explore the beauty of our planet. In recent times, Earth has become a focal point of interest throughout our universe because of the unique transition we are undergoing. Many beings have already been coming here to observe the transition and to enjoy the beauty of our planet from the skies. But once we complete our ascension to the New Earth, with its inherent pristine beauty, many more cosmic travelers will want to come here and learn first-hand about our experiences and explore the beauty of the New Earth 'up close and personal.'

Relationship with nature

Our relationship with nature will be dramatically different on the New Earth, compared to our current situation. As we emerge from duality and experience our Oneness with all of creation, our appreciation and respect for the animal, plant and mineral kingdoms will shift dramatically.

❖ Animals

We are gradually beginning to gain just an inkling of how profoundly our domestic pets have been assisting us, and how deeply we have underestimated their intelligence and abilities to communicate.

Indigenous cultures, such as the Native Americans, have historically had a much deeper understanding of, and respect for, *all* of the animals of our planet. They consider the animals to be their 'teachers,' both in regard to the qualities each species exhibits in their own life patterns, and also the manner in which the animals interact with humans, often conveying 'messages' through their appearance at important moments in our lives.

On the New Earth, animals will not need to serve as food for humans, and the killing of animals for sport will be perceived as an abhorrent chapter in the history of the human race. Within the awakening consciousness of the New Earth, a significant shift will take place in our rapport with the 'wild' animals of our planet. Such relationships will become similar to the manner in which we currently interact with our household pets, with mutual trust and respect.

And the way in which animals interact with each other will also undergo transformation. Species that historically have had predator/prey relationships with each other related to the 'food chain' will develop more loving and compassionate ways of interrelating. They, too, will experience the Oneness of all creation, and most likely will shift to a primarily agrarian diet.

❖ Plants

Throughout our history, there have always been a few gifted individuals who seem to have an uncanny ability to communicate with plants and inspire them to grow vigorously in response to feelings of love and appreciation expressed toward them. In the 1960's, Cleve Baxter used a polygraph machine to measure the reactions of plants to both positive and negative human emotions. Over the years, those ground-breaking experiments have been built upon by other researchers, adding layers of scientific credibility to what many of us have always sensed intuitively.

Certain individuals seem to be able to communicate directly with the consciousness of plants, learning from them how to honor their needs and preferences. Mystics have long known that plants (especially trees) are over-lighted by 'devas' which have a relationship with the plants similar to the relationship that a soul has with a human being.

On the New Earth, our normal relationships with plants and trees will be focused as much on their consciousness as on their physical qualities, resulting in a deepened level of mutual respect and appreciation.

❖ Minerals

Most of the interest related to the consciousness of the mineral kingdom has focused on crystals and gemstones. It has long been recognized that they are receptive to human thoughts and emotions, and that by working with the consciousness of crystals and gemstones, they can be used to greatly assist with healing processes.

However, all forms of minerals have consciousness. For example, spiritually-sensitive individuals have observed that rock formations, such as mountains, are over-lighted by devas with whom we can communicate in a manner similar to the devas of plants and trees.

❖ Water

The research work of Dr. Masaru Emoto has done much to awaken humanity to the consciousness of water, and the fact that it is especially sensitive to the thoughts and emotions of human beings. Subsequent research that is being done, especially in Eastern Europe, is continuing to add to our understanding of the essence of this magical substance that is in such abundance on our planet. It seems inevitable that our relationship with water on the New Earth will become much more appreciative and respectful.

❖ Nature spirits and elementals

Nature spirits, such as the fairies, gnomes, sprites, nymphs, undines and other elementals, work behind the scenes to support the nature kingdom in creating the exquisite beauty of our planet. Unfortunately the tendency on our present Earth has been to fictionalize these beings, relegating them to the worlds of children's stories. Thankfully, however, an increasing number of people – especially young people – are able to see and converse with these delightful nature spirits, learning from them how to live in closer harmony with the natural world.

As we emerge in the consciousness of the New Earth, it seems likely that nature spirits will become a normal part of our daily experiences, just as in today's world we are able to observe and appreciate the birds, the squirrels, and so many other delightful creatures.

Imagine –

We could continue to speculate on various other attributes of life on the New Earth. It would be difficult, however, to improve on the vision gifted to the world in 1971 by our beloved John Lennon –

Imagine there's no Heaven
It's easy if you try
No hell below us
Above us only sky
Imagine all the people
Living for today

Imagine there's no countries
It isn't hard to do
Nothing to kill or die for
And no religion too
Imagine all the people
Living life in peace

You may say that I'm a dreamer
But I'm not the only one
I hope someday you'll join us
And the world will be as one

Imagine no possessions
I wonder if you can
No need for greed or hunger
A brotherhood of man
Imagine all the people
Sharing all the world

You may say that I'm a dreamer
But I'm not the only one
I hope someday you'll join us
And the world will live as one

Chapter 18

Reuniting with Our 'Other Half'

When each of the original 144,000 Lightworkers came to Earth, our oversoul cluster was 'split' into two groups of 6 souls each. One of the groups of 6 came to Earth, and entered into the experience of duality as we began our service to the Light. The other group of 6 remained in the extraterrestrial worlds. That split continues to this day.

To better understand the nature of this split, which is sometimes referred to as a 'diagonal split,' let's return our focus to the image of 13 spheres that was discussed in Chapter 10. The image is repeated here for convenience. Imagine that an 'axis' passes through the center of one of the peripheral spheres,  then on through the center of the center sphere, and finally on through the center of the sphere on the opposite side. In this manner, we can see that there are 6 *'pairs'* of spheres that surround the center sphere.

A 'polarity' is involved in each of the 6 pairs of spheres. The nature of this polarity could best be described as 'yin' and 'yang,' or 'nurturing' and 'activating.' It is also closely related to the qualities of 'feminine' and 'masculine.'

When the cluster was split into two groups of 6, all of the 'yin' soul units ended up in one of the groups, and all of the 'yang' soul units ended up in the other. (In relating this back to the image of the 12 peripheral spheres, one can see why it would be referred to as a 'diagonal' split.)

Furthermore, of the 144,000 Lightworkers who came to Earth, exactly half came as the 'yin' aspect of their oversoul cluster, and the other half came as the 'yang' aspect. This provided a perfect yin-yang, or feminine-masculine balance within this group of Lightworkers.

As a point of clarification, if the aspect of us that came to Earth is the 'yin' aspect, this does not imply that we would always incarnate into a female body, or vice versa, if it was the 'yang' aspect of us that came to Earth. Virtually all of us have incarnated into both male and female bodies throughout our experiences here. But this may provide insight into why some Lightworkers emanate predominately a yin (nurturing) quality, while others emanate more of a yang (activating) quality, regardless of whether they are in a male or female body.

Future Selves – Twin Flames

All of us who are part of that original group of Lightworkers consequently retain an 'inner memory' that another half of us is 'out there somewhere.' We have an inherent longing within us to reconnect with the other half of our self so that we are able to feel 'whole' again. This will indeed happen as part of the ascension process, as we leave duality behind and enter into our new embodiment upon the 5th dimensional New Earth.

Because of our innate knowing of the plan for us to reconnect with our 'other half' at some point in the future, this part of us that is continuing to function in the extraterrestrial worlds is sometimes referred to as our 'future self.' However, the term 'future self' has been used by other spiritual writers and teachers in a variety of different contexts. For example, as we focus on making changes in the life of our 'current' self, we affect the nature of our self as it will be at a future point in time. In other words, we affect our 'future self.' Or another example, many of us sense that we have already lived lifetimes that are in 'future' time, relative to the present point in time here on Earth. So in this sense, the aspect of our self that has already lived that future lifetime could be thought of as a 'future self.'

The 'other half' of our self is also sometimes referred to as our 'Twin Flame,' This terminology is perhaps appropriate since there is, as we have just discussed, a yin-yang polarity that exists in the relationship with our other half. However, in this book we are somewhat cautious about using the term 'Twin Flame,' because it, too, has been used by so many different people to mean so many different things. For example,

110

some people have spent a lifetime hoping to meet their 'Twin Flame' in a human body here on Earth so that they can 'get married and live happily ever after.'

Anticipation of the imminent merging

As the time of the merging of the two halves of our self draws ever nearer, some of the Lightworkers who are involved in this situation seem to be developing a deeper awareness of the being that is an expression of their 'other half,' and are experiencing an enhanced linkage in consciousness with that being.

Chapter 19

The Intergalactic Federation

The 'Intergalactic Federation,' also sometimes known as the 'Federation of Light Worlds,' is an alliance that involves many, many celestial worlds throughout our universe. It operates in alignment with an impeccable ethical code, carrying out various missions as directed by the Spiritual Hierarchy. One of their primary roles is to maintain peace throughout our universe.

This Federation has been providing protection for our planet for eons of time, including protection from invasion by hostile forces. Due to the 'prime policy of non-interference,' which is fundamental to the evolutionary scheme of our universe, the Federation operates under certain constraints as to the types of protection that can be provided. For example, when the extraterrestrial race that is commonly referred to as the 'greys' negotiated with leaders of the United States many decades ago to provide technology in exchange for permission to build underground bases in this country, the Federation was not permitted to intervene, because this would have been interfering with the free will of inhabitants of Earth.

In the late 1940's, when the Creator of our universe issued the decree that inhabitants of Earth would not be permitted to use nuclear weapons in the conduct of warfare, the Intergalactic Federation was assigned the mission of preventing the use of nuclear weapons on our planet. Only within the past few years have a few brave 'whistleblowers' from within various military command structures stepped forward to publicly acknowledge that on many occasions throughout the past several decades, sizeable groups of nuclear weapons have mysteriously been disarmed. In many cases, spaceships have been observed in the vicinity of the related missile bases at the times the weapons were discovered to be disarmed. When the full scope of this effort is eventually revealed, we will realize how fortunate we have been to receive this measure of protection.

Some spaceships within the environs of Earth are not part of the Intergalactic Federation. Many of these are here simply observing the great shift that we are undergoing. In no case, however, are non-Federation ships permitted to interfere with the fulfillment of the Divine Plan for Earth. Appendix F provides a more detailed description of the various categories of ships that operate in the skies of Earth.

All spaceships are normally required to maintain 'cloaking' (invisibility) when functioning within the vicinity of Earth so as not to unduly alarm the citizens of Earth. However, as we know, they occasionally operate uncloaked for short periods of time to help raise our awareness of their presence.

The major world governments are fully aware of the existence of the extraterrestrial presence, and have repeatedly been contacted by beings of the Intergalactic Federation. But the world leaders have, for the most part, shunned the peaceful overtures of the Federation representatives, and have attempted to maintain a mantle of secrecy to protect their own selfish agendas. However, the cover-up is currently unraveling quite dramatically as an increasing number of brave officials who have functioned within the purview of the cover-up are risking recrimination, and are going public with their truth.

Also, the Federation is being permitted to increase the visibility of its presence. On several occasions their ships have appeared uncloaked over airports in various countries. In some cases, the airports, as a precautionary measure, shut down air traffic for several hours. These events have been widely reported through the internet, along with photographs, but in the United States, mainstream media still ignores these incidents.

Even now, as this book is being written, the likelihood of 'full disclosure' – open acknowledgment by the world leaders as to the existence of extraterrestrial – seems evermore close at hand. Once this announcement is made, it will clear the way for the Intergalactic Federation to make a public appearance simultaneously in countries all around the world. This so-called day of 'First Contact' will open the way for direct interaction with our brothers and sisters from the celestial realms.

Virtually overnight this will permit the extraterrestrials to share important new technologies with us, technologies that will include limitless clean energy, freeing humanity once and for all from our dependency on fossil fuels. They will also assist us in cleaning up all forms of pollution on our planet.

In addition, representatives of the Federation will provide information to the general public in all parts of the world as to the true history of our planet, including how we have been, and continue to be, manipulated by the 'power elite' of our world for the benefit of a 'privileged' few.

And very importantly, beings of the Federation will provide guidance and assistance that will facilitate our preparation for ascension.

In order for a planetary system to be eligible for membership in the Intergalactic Federation, it needs to have evolved to a state of consciousness and behavior that is consistent with the ethical standards under which the Federation operates. For obvious reasons, Earth is not yet a member. However, the New Earth will undoubtedly have extensive open involvement with the Federation. If all goes according to plan, it is likely that the New Earth will qualify for membership and be invited to join the Federation in the not-too-distant future.

On a personal note, it always feels strange to use the word 'extraterrestrials' or 'aliens' in referring to the beings who have come here in spaceships. In reality, they are no more 'extraterrestrial' or 'alien' than most of us who also have come here from the stars, but just happen to be in human bodies at this particular time. In fact, for a long time, various Lightworkers have been interacting on a non-physical level with beings of the Intergalactic Federation who are providing support for the fulfillment of the Divine Plan here on Earth.

Chapter 20

Preparation for Ascension

Throughout this book, we have discussed various aspects of ascension, including ways in which we may prepare for the ascension process. It might be helpful at this point to summarize some of the most important considerations.

Decision

Our decision to ascend to the New Earth needs to be made with clarity and resolve. Some people may feel more comfortable remaining in the 3rd dimensional world as they transition into the next evolutionary cycle, and that is perfectly okay. But if your choice is to move forward through ascension, then that decision needs to include a commitment to do the preparation that is required.

The decision regarding ascension is ultimately a personal decision, for each of us to make for our self. It is of value, of course, to discuss ascension with family members and friends. But the choice is too important to allow one's self to be swayed by what others may think, or by the choices they may make for themselves.

If one has children for whom they are responsible, it is important to know that infants or young children will make their decisions related to ascension within their souls. Most, if not all, already made their decision before entering into incarnation. If the children are older, then discussions with them would certainly be appropriate.

Ask for assistance

Once the decision is made, it is crucially important to ask for assistance in our preparation for ascension. Again, because of the principle of non-interference, those who are available to assist us from within the higher realms are not permitted to help us unless we ask for their assistance.

One of the most important roles that the Intergalactic Federation has taken on is to assist us with our preparation for ascension. That work has already quietly begun on a non-physical level. As soon as there is open interaction with the beings of the Federation, they will provide additional information about the ascension process, and will also provide direct assistance for those who have chosen the path of ascension.

Our physical body

It is important that we take action to cleanse and raise the frequency of our physical body. The guidelines and information provided in Chapter 7 can be very helpful in this regard.

Living a transcendent life

In Chapter 8, we discussed the importance of living a 'transcendent life.' Living such a life is important even if we do not choose the path of ascension, as it will significantly expand the options and possibilities available for our next life. Focusing on living a transcendent life, however, is absolutely essential if we have made the choice to ascend.

Preparation for ascension is primarily about raising the frequency of our body and our soul. Each interaction that we have with another person throughout our daily life can have only one of two possible outcomes:

- It *raises* the frequency of those involved.
- It *lowers* the frequency of those involved.

We don't need any special training in order to know the difference – we innately know whether an experience leaves us feeling uplifted or discouraged. The same is true of all experiences in life, whether it be watching a television program, or going for a walk in the woods.

The current ascension plan – 7 'waves'

It is our understanding that the current plan for ascension involves 7 distinct 'waves.' Some of those who ascend in the first wave will remain on the New Earth and work together on preparations for receiving those arriving in subsequent waves. However, some of those ascending in the first wave will return to our 3rd dimensional Earth for a period of time to assist others in their preparation.

It is not known at this time when the first wave will take place or how long it will take for all 7 waves to be completed. However, it appears likely that the interval between waves may be a matter of months, rather than days, with the entire process perhaps extending over a couple of years.

It is anticipated that the day of 'First Contact' with the beings of the Intergalactic Federation will take place before the first wave of ascension, so that they will be available to provide information and assistance to us related to ascension.

Chapter 21

Living Now in the New Consciousness

In Chapter 14, we discussed the process that Earth is going through at this time, with the Old Earth and New Earth both existing in the same 'space.' We may choose to align our self now with the Light grid and the consciousness of the New Earth, as the birthing of the New Earth proceeds. By our aligning with this evolving consciousness, we hasten the process. Again, an analogy would be helpful.

Imaginal cells

We are all familiar with the fact that through a process of metamorphosis, a caterpillar transforms into a butterfly. As scientists have studied this process more closely, they have discovered that the genesis of the caterpillar's transformation begins with the appearance within the caterpillar of what scientists have termed 'imaginal' cells. They are called this because they seem to hold within their genetic structure the 'image,' or 'blueprint' of the eventual butterfly. Researchers have no idea where these cells come from or what causes them to appear when they do.

At first, the imaginal cells are fought off and destroyed by the defense mechanism (immune system) of the caterpillar organism. But the imaginal cells keep coming back, and eventually form into clusters to strengthen their domain. Soon the clusters form bonds through which they pass genetic information to each other. The clusters resonate at a higher frequency than the host caterpillar, and they begin to change the physical make-up of the caterpillar.

At a certain point in the process, the long string of clustering imaginal cells seem to reach a 'critical mass' of influence whereby the caterpillar's destiny is altered, and the emergence of a butterfly is ultimately the result.

Our role related to the New Earth

Those of us who have chosen the pathway of ascension are like 'imaginal cells' – we carry within our consciousness a 'vision' of the New Earth. As we link together with other like-minded individuals who also are on the ascension path, we will eventually form a 'critical mass' that triggers the birthing of the New Earth. The future is in our hands and in our heart.

Living a transcendent life

Living a transcendent life is to live life as a fully integrated spiritual being in human form. At that point, we no longer struggle between our 'humanness' and our spiritual sense of purpose and direction. In fact, it is no longer even possible to distinguish between the two, we are simply One being, enjoying each moment of life as it unfolds from day to day.

Yes, we are still able to observe the human drama playing out on our planet, whether it be within our personal sphere of family and friends, or half way around the world. And we still have compassion for the seeming injustices and cruelties, with the resulting human pain and suffering. We still focus our efforts on helping to make this a better world. But, we no longer allow the 3rd dimensional drama to draw us into the turbulent emotional experiences that interfere with our heart-centered living.

At the beginning of this book, we wrote about the choice that is available to each of us: to ascend to a higher dimension along with Mother Earth at the end of this cycle, or to continue our evolutionary experiences in the 3rd dimensional realms. For those of us who have chosen the path of ascension, and who are inspired by the vision of life on the New Earth, it is perhaps only natural to want to persuade those whom we love to make a similar choice. But it is well to remember that whatever choice an individual soul makes will be a good choice for that particular soul.

Choosing love and joy

Love and joy are our natural states of being in the spiritual realms. So as we integrate our spiritual self with our human self, love and joy inherently become our natural states of being in the 'here and now' of our human experience here on Earth. This is what it means to live a transcendent life, and this is what it means to become a 'galactic human.'

Appendix

Appendix A

Insights Related to Heart Transplants

One of the fascinating aspects of recent discoveries related to the heart-brain involves the experiences of people who have undergone heart transplants. Let's consider a few.

In her 1998 book, *A Change of Heart*,[14] author Claire Sylvia describes how after a successful heart-lung transplant, she found herself craving new foods and beverages, experiencing a significantly enhanced libido, and generally feeling as though a new personality had somehow fused with her own. She also began to have recurring dreams about a young man named Tim, who she believed to be the organ donor. In spite of medical confidentiality rules, Claire eventually was able to discover the identity of the donor and made contact with the donor's family. They confirmed that her new cravings and personality characteristics were the same as those of the deceased young donor, an 18-year old man named Tim, who had been killed in a motorcycle accident.

Gaea Shaw had been a school teacher for 27 years when her health began to fail. She was diagnosed as having a heart condition, and for 6 years, in spite of efforts to treat her medically, she felt her life force continue to diminish. In her book, *Dying to Live*,[15] she describes how time seemed to be running out for her when she was finally listed for a heart transplant. Good fortune was in her favor, and a heart became available. The operation was successful, but she needed to embark on an exercise program to begin to rebuild her strength and stamina. She had never been a swimmer, but felt strongly guided to be in the water. Her first efforts were excruciating, but with help from the lifeguard, her swimming ability soon improved remarkably. The lifeguard became her coach, and she went on to win gold medals at subsequent special Olympics.

She later had an opportunity to meet the parents of the heart donor, a 15-year old boy named Christopher who had been struck and killed by an automobile. As she learned about Christopher's life, she was told by his parents that, among other things, he had always had a passion for swimming.

Other heart recipients have reported similar experiences. Paul Pearsall is a psychologist. In his book, *The Heart's Code*,[16] he describes some of the experiences of people who have undergone organ transplants. One particularly interesting case involves what he refers to as 'domino transplantation.' Doctors have found that in certain cases, a person who is in need of a lung transplant has a much better chance of survival if both the heart and lung from the donor are transplanted simultaneously. In such cases, the heart of the transplant recipient is then available for transplantation into a patient needing a heart transplant.

In the particular case that he describes, he identifies the recipient of the heart and lung transplant as Jim, and the subsequent recipient of Jim's heart as Fred. Dr. Pearsall had an opportunity to interview both Jim and Fred, along with their respective wives, Sandra and Karen, several months after the transplants took place. During the interview, Fred told Jim of new food cravings he had experienced since receiving Jim's heart, and Jim verified that these had, indeed, been some of his favorite foods. They also talked about changes in personality temperaments that both had experienced since the transplants. Prior to the transplants, Jim had been a 'Type A' personality, very intense and temperamental. Since the heart and lung transplant (from an unknown donor), Jim had become much calmer, but also frequently depressed. On the other hand, Fred, who had always been easy going and carefree, had become much more hyperactive and temperamental since receiving Jim's heart.

Sometime after the interview, Dr. Pearsall was able to trace the identity of the donor of the heart and lungs that Jim had received, a young woman. Her family said that she had always been shy and soft-spoken, and that she frequently suffered from depression. In fact, she had taken her own life in despair over a lost love.

There is more to the story. As the two couples became more comfortable with each other during the interview, Karen talked about another change she experienced in Fred after the heart transplant. She said that Fred often called her 'Sandy' during the passion of their lovemaking. Understandably, Karen was disturbed by this, but when she would question Fred about it, he would always deny having called her by that name. Somewhat embarrassed at this point, Jim's wife, Sandra, acknowledged that although Jim normally called her 'Sandra,' he had a habit of calling her 'Sandy' during their lovemaking.

What do these stories suggest about the human heart?

With this very limited anecdotal evidence, it would be naïve to draw any specific conclusions. It is an area in which credible research could prove to be very insightful. However, these stories do suggest some interesting possibilities as to the role of the heart-brain related to:

- Personality characteristics
- Feelings about people
- Food preferences
- Activity preferences

They also suggest that when we make reference to the 'desires of the heart,' we may well be referring to information and feelings that are stored within our heart-brain. Sometimes common sayings carry wisdom that goes unnoticed by our cognitive mind. For example, when we say "I love you from the bottom of my heart," are we really referring to our heart-brain which resides primarily in the fatty tissue at the base of the heart? These are interesting possibilities to ponder.

Appendix B

Unique Nature of Interstitial Zones

The word 'interstitial' means 'in-between.' So when we refer to 'interstitial zones,' we are referring to that which exists between two states of being. In this sense, an interstitial zone could be thought of as a 'transition zone.'

In our discussions about intuition in Chapter 4, we referred to the transition between being asleep and being awake. This in-between state is an interstitial zone, as depicted in the diagram below.

Sleep / Wakefulness

In the in-between state in which we are still partially asleep and just beginning to awaken, we seem to have the ability to be partially in touch with elements of both states of being, and we can drift back and forth between the two. We may have awareness of 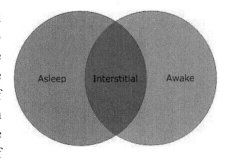 remnants of a dream that was part of our sleep-state experience. Perhaps subtle thoughts or ideas pop up from some unknown place. So long as we don't focus our conscious mind too sharply on them, they seem to have a life of their own and sometimes gently lead us to other possibilities. In that interstitial state of awareness, we seem to know that we can navigate closer to wakefulness, or we can also allow our self to drift back into a sleep state.

As we are learning to access deeper levels of our intuition, this interstitial zone is rich with possibilities. Through experience, we can learn to linger in this zone for extended periods of time. The trick is to retain the seed-thoughts (intuitive flashes) that percolate out of this in-between state of being. The act of writing them down or recording them with a voice recorder usually brings us too far over into the wakeful state, making it difficult to return to the interstitial zone. But we can learn to engage the conscious mind just enough to capture the seed-thoughts as they arise, and then when we feel 'complete,' we can gently move into wakefulness and jot down or record keywords so that we do not lose the thoughts or ideas.

Daylight / Darkness

Another example of an interstitial zone would be the transition from daylight to darkness (dusk), or darkness to daylight (dawn). One of the characteristics of interstitial zones is their serendipitous unpredictability. If one had only experienced the fullness of the noonday sun and the darkness of the midnight hour, one could not possibly anticipate the grandeur of a sunset or a sunrise that can emerge within the interstitial zones between daylight and darkness. The richness of a sunset or sunrise makes full daylight or full darkness seem a bit boring by comparison.

Unpredictability seems to reign in interstitial zones. How many times have we been in a beautiful natural setting, such as the mountains or by the ocean, and waited at dusk or dawn with camera in hand, ready to capture the glorious kaleidoscope of colors? Sometimes our anticipation and patience are rewarded, while at other times the display is disappointing. Or there may be situations in which we have been preoccupied with activity as dusk approaches, and suddenly the sky breaks out in a magnificent color and light show. It seems almost impossible to predict.

We are affected by the transition from daylight to darkness, or vice versa, in other ways as well. The Earth energies tend to be more magnetic in nature at dawn, and more electric at dusk. Our feelings and emotions tend to resonate more with magnetic energies, while our thoughts tend to be more electric in nature. Consequently, the interstitial zone that we call dusk is more conducive to insightful mental activity, while dawn provides us an opportunity to delve more deeply into our feelings and emotions.

With this in mind, let me describe a process that one of my mentors, Dr. Derald Langham, shared with me. He was involved with a small group of people who got together fairly regularly to explore various aspects of science or philosophy, reminiscent of the days of Plato and Socrates. He was aware of the potential of interstitial zones, and over time evolved a process to capture the richness of the zone between daylight and darkness. The group would meet at his home about an hour before dusk and begin to have a conversation. They would leave all of the lights in his home turned off, so there would only be the diminishing daylight coming in from the outside. As dusk gently enfolded the group, the conversation began to grow richer, eventually continuing on in full darkness.

Other interstitial-related principles had also been incorporated into their process, such as the zone between talking and silence. In so much of our contemporary conversation, people tend to become uncomfortable if there are long pauses. By encouraging periods of silence within a group conversation, however, it provides a fertile environment for new and insightful ideas to emerge.

Seasons

As one begins to relate to life in the context of interstitial zones, we start to recognize them everywhere! For example, instead of thinking of the annual weather cycles as consisting of the four seasons – winter, spring, summer and autumn – we might consider just the two extremes: winter, the peak of dormancy and bleakness, and summer, the peak of the fullness of nature. From this perspective, spring becomes an interstitial zone between winter and summer, and autumn an interstitial zone between summer and winter.

Just as a beautiful sunrise is a peak experience between darkness and daylight, so also the 'interstitial zone' that we call spring – with new growth and blossoms springing forth everywhere – is a peak experience between winter and summer. Similarly, the magnificent beauty of autumn colors exemplifies the interstitial zone between summer and winter.

Land/Water – Plains/Mountains

We could also associate the concept of interstitial zones with geographical features. For example, we could think of a seashore or lakeshore as an interstitial zone between land and water. Isn't it interesting that people are drawn to live in such areas. The middle of an ocean is really quite boring, at least for most of us; so also are the endless plains of the mid-lands of our country. But in the interstitial zones where land and water meet, all of the resplendent beauty of our beaches and rugged shorelines delight our senses.

Likewise, one finds relatively few people living on the flat plains of eastern Colorado or in the ruggedness of the Colorado Rockies. However, millions of people are drawn to live where the plains and mountains meet, along the so-called 'front range' that extends from Colorado Springs on the south, to Fort Collins on the north. What is it about our inherent nature that draws us to such interstitial zones?

The dynamics of '3-ness'

Much research has been done to explore the differences between the ways our right-brain and left-brain function. Since the educational systems in the Western world tend to focus mostly on left-brain types of cognitive learning, considerable interest has been focused on developing techniques to help people achieve a better balance between their left-brain and right-brain thinking processes. Again, we might look at this in terms of learning ways to spend more of our time in the interstitial zone between left-brain and right-brain activity.

With the emergence of awareness of the 'heart-brain,' a third element has been introduced into our thinking model. If we consider this model in terms of interstitial zones, we realize that in addition to the interstitial zone between the left-brain and right-brain, there is also an interstitial zone between the left-brain and the heart-brain, and another such zone between the right-brain and heart-brain. This is depicted in the diagram. In the very center is an area we have labeled the 'dynamic center.'

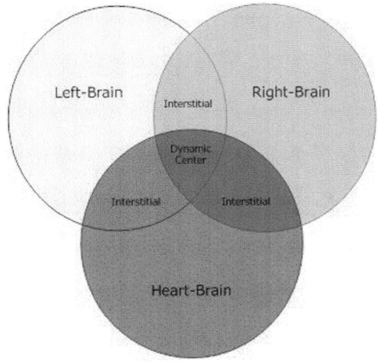

This dynamic center represents an interstitial zone involving three attributes, rather than two. Much of life in the natural world involves an interplay between three variables. For example, in electricity, Ohm's law defines the relationship between *voltage, resistance* and *current*. The principles of thermodynamics involve the relationship between *pressure, temperature* and *volume*. The dynamics of plant growth involve interaction of *moisture, temperature* and *light*. In the mechanics of motion, *force* equals *mass* times *acceleration*.

Nikola Tesla, who invented ways to generate and utilize alternating current, designed the 3-phase system that is still the standard for today's commercial electrical systems. Using this system, he was able to create a rotating electromagnetic induction field that is used in electric motors. This is another example of how '3-ness' is involved in the creation of

135

dynamic motion. So when we are dealing interstitial zones that involve three aspects rather than two, the combined interstitial zones result in a much more dynamic environment.

The science of interstitial zones

A brief discussion of the science that is involved with interstitial zones may be helpful. For the purpose of contrast, let's start with the concept of binary logic, upon which virtually all of today's digital computers are based. In binary logic, only one of two states can exist: 'on' or 'off.' This is similar to a normal light switch that we have in our homes. In reference to the interstitial diagrams we have been using, it would consist of two circles that touch each other, but which do not overlap. For example in the 'awake' or 'asleep' situation, if we are sleeping soundly and a loud alarm clock goes off, we shift immediately to the 'awake' state, with virtually no 'in-between.'

In contrast to binary logic, let's consider analog logic, sometimes referred to as 'fuzzy' logic. Analog logic is based on the concept of 'gradations.' Returning to the analogy of a light switch in our home, analog logic is like a 'dimmer' switch; the light can not only be off or on, but also exhibit 'gradations' in-between, ranging from very dim to very bright. Interstitial zones are gradational by their very nature – partly one thing, partly another. It is the 'partly' aspect that makes them so unpredictable and so rich with possibilities.

Living between worlds

In this book, we have discussed the great shift we are undergoing as we progress through the stages of ascension from a 3rd-dimensional reality to a 5th-dimensional world. We are already living in the interstitial zone between these two dimensional realities. Just as in the interstitial zone between sleep and wakefulness we can shift back and forth between the two states of consciousness, many of us are now finding ourselves subtly shifting back and forth in consciousness between 3rd-dimensional and 5th-dimensional realities.

The Seven Chakras

Chakras are energy centers that link our energy body with our physical form. They have long been an important element in Eastern religious teachings as well as in esoteric mystical traditions. The body has 7 primary chakras, each of which functions in conjunction with one of the glands of the endocrine system. Energies functioning through the chakras are sensed by the receptor cells in the corresponding endocrine gland, which in turn transmits related information to the neural networks in the sensory centers of the body. The endocrine gland also secretes appropriate hormones in response to the energies received through the chakra.

There are additional chakras above the head and at other locations external to the body, and there are also energy centers at other locations throughout the body, but those are beyond the scope of our present consideration. The 7 major chakras are as follows.

Crown chakra

The crown chakra is like an energy cone that extends upward and outward from the top of the head. It may be thought of as our spiritual connection to the higher realms. The crown chakra acts in conjunction with the pineal gland, which is the 'master gland' of the endocrine system. Although the pineal gland functions primarily through the other endocrine glands, it itself secretes melatonin and serotonin which are related to the circadian rhythms of the body.

Brow chakra

The brow chakra extends outward toward the front from a point midway between and slightly above the eye brows. The focal point of this chakra is directed inward toward the photo-receptor cells of the pituitary gland. This chakra is traditionally referred to by the mystics as the 'third eye,' because this is the seat of our inner vision (clairvoyance).

Throat chakra

As its name implies, the throat chakra is located in the throat area of the body. It is bi-directional, extending out toward the front and also out toward the back. It is associated with the thyroid gland. Mystics associate the throat chakra with the function of clairaudience (inner hearing). It also is related to creative expression.

Heart chakra

The heart chakra is located in the center of the chest in the vicinity of the heart. It can be viewed as a 'link-pin,' linking the upper three 'spiritual' chakras with the lower three 'human' chakras. Like the throat chakra, it is bi-directional, extending both to the front and to the rear of the body. It is associated with the thymus gland, which plays a key role in the immune system.

Solar Plexus chakra

The solar plexus chakra is located at the solar plexus, which is about 2 inches above the naval. It is referred to by the mystics as the 'power center' of the body. The solar plexus is also our emotional center. This chakra is associated with the two adrenal glands, with one located just above each kidney. The adrenal glands are related to the energy reserve system of the body and play an active role in the 'fight or flight' response.

Sexual chakra

The sexual chakra is located in the lower abdomen and is associated with the gonads (testicles in the male and ovaries in the female). The sexual chakra plays an important role in our reproductive instincts. It is also associated with the sexual pleasure centers of the body (penis in the male and clitoris in the female).

Base chakra

The base chakra is located at the base of the spine (sacrum). This chakra is a grounding force that enables us to connect to the Earth energies and empower our being. It is closely related to the survival instincts of the body and also our ability to be 'present' in the here and now.

Appendix D

Mind-to-Mind Communication

Our crown chakra is our primary communication gateway to beings in other realms. This chakra functions in conjunction with the pineal gland, which is located in the center of our head, at the top of the brain stem. It is connected to the cerebellum through a 'stalk,' as may be seen in the diagram on the next page.

The pineal gland has two parts. One part is involved with the production and secretion melatonin and serotonin, and the other part is associated with sensory aspects. The internal layer of the sensory part is heavily populated with photo-receptor cells, similar to those found in the retina of the eyes. The nerve fibers extending from these photo-receptor cells pass down through the connective stalk and terminate in the cerebellum.

Information that we receive through the crown chakra is in the form of encoded Light. As it is sensed by the photo-receptor cells in the pineal gland, the information travels down through the associated nerve fibers to the cerebellum, where it is decoded and processed.

The functioning of the cerebellum has not been researched as extensively as the cerebral hemispheres. However, one of the functions of the cerebellum has to do with the fine tuning of motor responses. Damage to the cerebellum does not cause muscular paralysis, but it does inhibit smooth and coordinated movements. We believe that the cerebellum is deeply involved in kinetic memory and precise muscle movements that are used in artistic expression, such as playing a musical instrument, painting a picture, or sculpting.

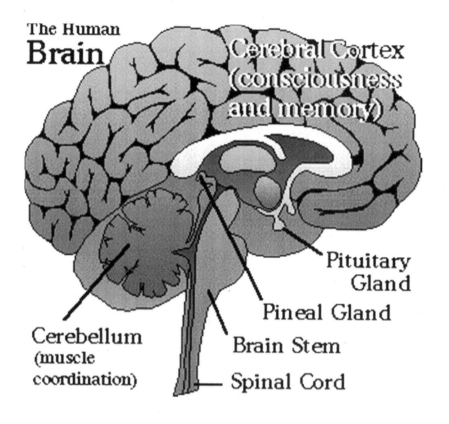

The Human
Brain

Cerebral Cortex
(consciousness
and memory)

Pituitary
Gland

Pineal Gland

Cerebellum
(muscle
coordination)

Brain Stem

Spinal Cord

Since medical science does not yet acknowledge the existence of the chakras, very little research has been done on what happens within the cerebellum to the signals received through the nerve fibers that extend from the photo-receptor cells in the pineal gland. Since these nerve fibers terminate in the cerebellum, we can only assume that part of the cerebellum functions similarly to the sensory cortex areas in the cerebrum, which processes nerve impulses received through our five senses. Also, the cerebellum is connected to each of the cerebral hemispheres through the cortico-ponto cerebellar tracts. Therefore, information arriving in the cerebellum via the crown chakra and pineal gland is most likely sent on to the cerebral hemispheres for further interpretation and processing.

To summarize, we believe that when a psychically sensitive person 'channels' information from a being within the higher realms, the 'information' is received in the form of encoded Light through the crown chakra and converted to nerve impulses by the photo-receptor cells in the pineal gland. The nerve impulses are decoded within the cerebellum, and the corresponding information is sent on to the cerebral hemi-spheres (left-brain and right-brain) for further interpretation and processing – for example, converting the information into thoughts and words.

Additionally, we believe this interdimensional information stream may be supplemented with corresponding information received through the brow ('third eye') chakra in the form of images (clairvoyance), and the throat chakra in the form of auditory sensations (clairaudience).

From our perspective, one of the important conclusions that can be drawn from all of this is that the information coming to us through the crown, brow and throat chakras is all received and processed within the brain and glandular structures in the head. This is in contrast to *intuitive* information, which is received and processed in the area of the heart.

Appendix E

Accessing Consciousness

Consciousness is the 'language' of our Higher Self. It is beyond words, beyond thoughts. When we are able to access consciousness, it comes to us as 'knowingness,' or as 'awareness.'

As our spiritual awakening and transformation progress, we gradually develop the ability to tune into and be receptive to the consciousness of our Higher Self, and eventually to the consciousness of the 'ALLNESS THAT IS.' At that point, no consciousness anywhere in Creation is beyond our accessibility. The consciousness of a tree or a bird, or even the consciousness of a rock is available to us. Life then has the potential to become more expansive than we can possibly imagine.

The essence of consciousness is *Light, encoded Light.* It is similar to the encoded light that we receive through our crown chakra, except that it is of a higher 'octave.' Although consciousness interacts with the realm of our time-space reality, its essence resides at a more refined level of existence.

Golden Column

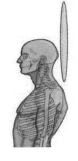

Although it is not yet well known or understood, there is a 'Golden Column' that is associated with our soul. It extends upward from the top of our spinal column as illustrated in diagram. The Golden Column serves as an 'antenna' for receiving and sending the encoded Light frequencies of consciousness.

We believe that the heart-brain plays a key role in the decoding and processing of the modulated Light that is associated with consciousness. Unfortunately, with the discovery of the heart-brain being so relatively recent, we do not have the advantage of extensive research about the heart-brain in the way that we do for the brain in our head. We do believe that there are parallels between the way Light is received through the Crown chakra, sensed by the Pineal gland, and then decoded and processed by the Cerebellum, and the way that Light is received, sensed, and ultimately processed by the heart-brain. So we are going to explain it from that frame of reference, believing that the concept is correct, and yet knowing that corrections and refinements will arise in the future as research progresses.

Thymus Gland

As indicated in the chakra information in Appendix C, the endocrine gland that is associated with the heart chakra is the thymus gland. Up until about the 1960's, medical science believed that the primary role of the thymus was related to the growth process in the early stages of life. The developing thymus gland is at its largest size in relation to the size of the rest of the body at about the age of two years. It is at its largest absolute size around the age of puberty. Historically it was believed that from puberty on, it was normal for the thymus to gradually diminish in size throughout life. In fact, it was questioned whether or not the thymus gland actually had a useful role in the functioning of the human body after puberty.

Then, about 50 years ago, medical science began to discover the crucial role the thymus plays in the development and active functioning of the immune system. From that point on, most of the research that has been focused on the thymus has related to the immune system, including the lymphatic system.

However, we believe that the thymus also plays a key role related to the Golden Column, in the same way that the pineal gland plays an essential role related to the crown chakra. We also believe that someday it will be discovered that there are photo-receptor cells located in the thymus very similar to the photo-receptor cells in the pineal gland.

The diagram below shows the two lobes of the thymus gland nestled around the upper part of the heart. It also shows a sizeable glandular unit at the top of each lobe of the thymus which is labeled "Cervical extension of the thymus." But we have not yet been able to find any information about the nature or the functions of these thymus extensions.

In the anatomical structure of the body these units are located just behind the *manubrium*, which is the top part of the sternum. In fact, the top part of these cervical extensions tend to protrude slightly above the manubrium. If we relate this diagram to the previous diagram of the Golden Column, it is evident that these two cervical extensions are at about the same level as the bottom of the Golden Column. So we are strongly suspicious that it may be within these two units that the photo-receptor cells are located. If this is true, we would expect to find nerve fibers extending from these two units and terminating somewhere in the heart-brain.

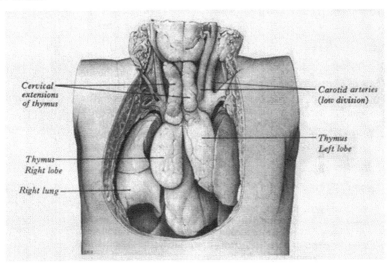

Levels of Consciousness

As we evolve and become increasingly adept at accessing the consciousness of our Higher Self, we have an opportunity to learn to access consciousness beyond that of our Higher Self as well. While we understand little about the nature of consciousness, there seem to be 'levels' or 'bands' as shown in the diagram on the next page. The most easily accessible band is the consciousness of our Higher Self, shown at the bottom of the diagram. We have already discussed this at some length, so let's move to the next level in the chart, which we have labeled "Inter-Specie & Intra-Specie Consciousness."

For many years, Rupert Sheldrake, a British biologist, has been studying the manner in which individual animals within a species seem to learn behavioral habits from each other even when they are separated by significant distances, and thus have no opportunity to physically observe each other's behavior. This phenomenon is sometimes referred to as the 'hundredth monkey effect,' based on a story first reported in the mid-1970s. In this story, a scientist observed that a learned new behavior within a group of monkeys in one part of the world seemed to spread rapidly to monkeys of the same species in other parts of the world, once a critical number of monkeys had learned the new behavior.

| "ALLNESS-THAT-IS" CONSCIOUSNESS |
| UNIVERSAL CONSCIOUSNESS |
| INTER-SPECIE INTRA-SPECIE CONSCIOUSNESS |
| HIGHER SELF CONSCIOUSNESS |

In Sheldrake's work, he postulated the idea of a 'morphogenetic' field through which animals within the same species seem to be in communication with each other. This might also explain how a flock of birds flying together in tight formation seems to maneuver through the air as though they are a single unit.

We believe that Sheldrake's morphogenetic field is essentially a field of 'consciousness' through which individual animals of the same species are in constant communication with each other. And we would postulate that the manner in which this communication takes place is a process similar to the one we described related to the Golden Column.

We know that certain people seem to be gifted with an uncanny ability to communicate directly with animals. This is especially true in regard to people communicating with their domestic animals, such as a cat, a dog, or a horse. For some people, this communication ability seems to extend to animals even when no personal relationship exists, such as with animals in the wild. Other people seem to be similarly gifted in their abilities to communicate with a plant or tree, or even a crystal. All living forms have consciousness, and we believe that everyone has the potential capacity to tap into this consciousness through the facility of their Golden Column.

The third band on the chart is labeled 'Universal Consciousness.' By this we are referring to all consciousness within our universe. Whether through the perspective of traditional astronomy or through a more esoteric perspective such as presented in Itzhak Bentov's book, *Stalking the Wild Pendulum: On the Mechanics of Consciousness*, universes seems to be important 'building blocks' of the Cosmos. We believe that as our awareness expands and extends out into our universe and beyond, we will find that tapping into any and all consciousness within a universe is the next natural step in the progression.

Finally, the ultimate step would be to learn to tap into the consciousness of the 'ALLNESS THAT IS,' which would be the consciousness of all of Creation.

Appendix F

Spaceships in Our Skies

As we have previously discussed, extraterrestrial beings and their spaceships currently reside in the environs of Earth. Our focus has been primarily on those of the Intergalactic Federation. However, several other categories of spaceships also operate in the skies of Earth. Following is a brief summary.

Intergalactic Federation

The Intergalactic Federation, sometimes also referred to as the Galactic Federation or the Federation of Light Worlds, is an alliance of highly evolved extraterrestrial worlds that operates in alignment with a very strict code of ethics. They function in close cooperation with the spiritual hierarchies, and are carrying out an important mission here on Earth at this time. The ships retain the identity of their celestial system of origin, such as the Pleiades or Sirius, but function under the auspices of the Federation.

These ships are of a wide range of sizes and designed for various purposes. 'Motherships' are huge, and contain within them everything that one would find in a modern city, including landscape features. They are designed for long-term travel and residency, and carry within them all of the 'comforts of home.' Because of their size, they are not permitted to come close to Earth, as they could be destabilizing to Earth's structure and energy field. They serve as a base of operations for smaller ships. Many of the medium and smaller size ships are designed for specific functions, such as medical support, scientific labs, or policing functions.

Extraterrestrial Non-Federation Ships

Ships are here from many different star systems that are not associated with the Intergalactic Federation. Travel throughout space is somewhat like travel on the open seas here on Earth; ships are permitted to travel freely so long as they do not interfere with other ships or with the affairs of Earth. Again, this is analogous to respecting 'territorial waters' when traveling on the open seas.

There are two primary reasons why so many such ships are here at this time. First, the nature of the ascension plan that is unfolding here on Earth is unique – it has never happened in this way before anywhere in our universe. Secondly, because Earth is such a beautiful planet, many ships are here on what are essentially 'sight-seeing' trips.

Ships of the Inner Earth Beings

As we are approaching the end of this evolutionary cycle, the beings of inner Earth, that were discussed earlier in this book, are reaching out to re-establish a relationship with the surface civilization. At the time of this writing, a very interesting video is available on YouTube – an interview of Drunvalo Melchizedek by Lilou Mace[9] that includes pictures of these ships. These particular ships are referred to as 'plasma' ships because of their amber glow.

Ships from Earth's future

The vast majority of spaceships have the ability to travel through time to the 'past' or 'future.' Some of the ships that are operating in our skies are ships that have traveled here from 'future time' on Earth.

Ships of the secret military

For the past several decades, the 'secret military' of our planet has been reverse-engineering spaceship technology from extraterrestrial spaceships that have crashed on Earth. Because of the veil of secrecy that surrounds this endeavor, the numbers and types of these ships that are currently operational are not known. However, it is highly likely that numerous ships of this type are operating in our skies.

Acknowledgments and References

Acknowledgments

The perspectives and information in this book have come from a lifetime of learning. The contributions of innumerable friends, family members and fellow travelers on the spiritual path are woven throughout the pages. To attempt to mention all of them would be a book in itself. Yet, to single out only a few would be to omit others. So let me just express my deep appreciation to all of you!

References

1. Institute of HeartMath, 14700 West Park Avenue, Boulder Creek, CA 95006. Websites: heartmath.org and heartmath.com.

2. Interview with Drunvalo Melchizedek by Lilou Mace, (video - Part 2), January 2011, Lilou's Juicy Living Tour, Websites: JuicyLivingTour.com & YouTube.com.

3. Gary Null, Ph.D.; Carolyn Dean, MD, ND; Martin Feldman, MD; Debora Rasio, MD; Dorothy Smith, Ph.D.; *Death by Medicine*. December 2003.

4. Andreas Moritz. *The Amazing Liver and Gallbladder Flush*. Landrum, South Carolina, 2007. Website: Ener-Chi.com.

5. Dr. Hans Hertel and Dr. Bernard H. Blanc, Swiss Federal Institute of Technology and University Institute for Biochemistry, 1992. Court ruling: European Court of Human Rights, 1998.

6. Ruth Montgomery. *Strangers Among Us*. Fawcett: (Paperback) 1984.

7. Rosalie Heart. *Awaken*. Balboa Press, Bloomington, Indiana, 2011. Website: balboapress.com.

8. Archangel Michael, through Carolyn Evers. *Earth History: Past, Present & Future*. Cosmic Connections, 2006.

9. Interview with Drunvalo Melchizedek by Lilou Mace. Plasma Beings (video - Part 2). Websites: Drunvalo.net & Juicy Living Tour.com & YouTube.com.

10. Nancy Ann Tappe. *Understanding Your Life Through Color.* Aquila Libris Publishing Company, 2009.

11. Doreen Virtue, Ph.D. *Indigo, Crystal and Rainbow Children* (2-CD audio). Hay House, Inc. 2005. Website: hayhouse.com.

12. Dianne Lancaster. *Anger and the Indigo Child.* Wellness Press, Boulder, Colorado, 2002.

13. Paul Hawken. *Blessed Unrest.* Penguin Group, New York, 2007.

14. Claire Sylvia. *A Change of Heart.* Little, Brown & Company, New York, 1997.

15. Gaea Shaw. *Dying to Live.* Pilgrim's Process, Inc., Longmont, Colorado, 2005.

16. Paul Pearsall, Ph.D. *The Heart's Code.* Broadway Books, New York, 1998.